Elementary Price Theory

Benjamin Ward

ELEMENTARY
PRICE THEORY

The Free Press, New York
Collier-Macmillan Limited, London

Collier-Macmillan Canada, Ltd., Toronto, Ontario

Library of Congress Catalog Card Number: 67-15673

First Printing

Preface

Within the last five years there has been a tremendous increase in the number of inexpensive paperbacks available for use in the principles course. These books now offer the instructor great flexibility in constructing a course that fits both the needs of his students and his own competence and interests. They also provide the opportunity to supplement and complement some of the less satisfactory parts of standard texts. The present book is offered for these uses in the area of price theory. It attempts to provide a concise, modern statement of the theory at a level suitable for serious beginning students. In addition to covering traditional topics considerable attention has been devoted to risk, information, bargaining and government decision making.

The reader should not expect to find many new ideas in an elementary text; however in a number of places he may find that the style of presentation is novel. The exposition has profited greatly from the careful reading and numerous suggestions of Professors Procter Thompson of Clarement Men's College, Clifton M. Grubbs of the University of Texas, and an anonymous referee. Much help has also been derived from the comments of teaching assistants and students at Berkeley during the course of a half dozen presentations of much of the material. Only the author is responsible for whatever errors and obscurities may remain.

Benjamin Ward

Contents

CONTENTS

1

Economics and the Economy

The field of economics has traditionally been concerned with the problems connected with managing the social activities of production, distribution, and consumption. The origins of the field are deeply rooted in practical questions. Ancient treatises were primarily concerned with estate management, with the sale and purchase of crops and slaves, the organization of field work and the like. In early modern times the central concern of much economic writing had shifted to the management of the emerging national state, to the role of money and of exports and imports in promoting the wealth and power of the citizenry and the state. By the end of the nineteenth century a third problem was being systematically explored: the interaction among all the various participants in a modern economy and its consequences in terms of the kinds and amounts of goods produced, the manner of their production, and their allocation among consumers. All these problems and a number of others continue to be of interest to economists; however, this book deals primarily with the last of the three.

The economic theory of resource allocation, often called price theory for short, deals with interaction among participants in an economy. Yet it deals with a good deal more than that, and in fact

Economics and Decisions

1

the theory is not organized around the idea of interaction. Each participant, each unit in an economy has a management task to face: it has control over some resources and must determine the appropriate way to make use of them; and management consists essentially in the making of a series of decisions. As a consequence the decision has become the organizing concept of price theory.

The decisions that interest economists are those concerned with goods and services.

> ► *Goods and services are those things and activities that are or can be traded on markets*[1]

Definitions like this one which aim at setting limits to a field of inquiry should not be taken too seriously. They can serve to give a general insight into the kinds of problems that are relevant for the field but do not determine rigid boundaries. Clearly bread, automobiles, and haircuts are goods and services under the definition. A slightly less obvious case would be the corn grown by a farmer and fed by him to his cow. This would qualify because the corn might sold on a market even though it is not. A more doubtful case would be the activity of child raising. Though this is normally carried out by parents, the existence of nurses, governesses, military schools and the like shows that all or most of the activities associated with child raising can be bought and sold on a market. Nevertheless economists have never attempted to include the economic value of child raising in their measures of the value of output.

Other aspects of decisions than their relation to goods and services serve to restrict the scope of economics. For example, not all decisions are interesting subjects of analysis. The interesting decisions are hard decisions, those in which the right choice is not immediately obvious. A property that all hard decisions have in common is that they require compromise. If the decision is a hard one, you must give up some of one thing you want in order to get more of some other thing you want. Some examples of different kinds of hard decisions will illustrate this point.

1. In some decisions the only alternatives available are very distasteful. For example, a gentleman must either fight a duel with an expert or be branded a coward. Or an unemployed man after long search is finally offered work that he hates.

2. The alternatives available may be very different so that comparison is difficult. A young man shows great promise both as a violinist

1. The symbol ► before a sentence indicates that it contains an important definition. Two such symbols, ► ►, indicate an important proposition, the conclusion drawn from an argument.

and as a boxer. A voter must choose between a candidate who has a good foreign policy but a bad domestic policy, and his opponent who supports the opposite policies.

3. Some alternatives may be very uncertain in their consequences. Our duelist is allowed to choose between a fight to the death and a game of Russian roulette. An investor must decide which assets to buy in an uncertain market.

4. Some uncertain alternatives may become less uncertain if time and effort is spent collecting further information about them. Then an initial choice must be faced: whether to decide now or to wait and collect more information. This decision probably must be made in connection with all the above examples.

All social sciences are concerned with human decision making. However, economics probably has the most highly developed, integrated body of theory of any of the social sciences. The principal reason for this is that there is a means ready to hand for greatly reducing the "hardness" of most hard economic decisions. This means consists in the development of a common measure of the value of many properties of most of the alternatives faced by economic decision makers. Price is this measure, and

▶ *Price theory, the subject of this book, is the study of the reasons for and the consequences of using prices in economic decision making, and of the means by which prices are determined.*

Because prices usually are generated on markets we will spend a good deal of time studying the ways in which markets operate. But because prices can be generated without recourse to markets, price theory is really more general than the theory of markets. As a consequence price theory comes close to being the same thing as the theory of resource allocation.

The role of price as a measure of economic value stems from its relation to scarcity. Goods and services of economic interest are scarce goods—that is, more of them are wanted by people than can be made available without effort or cost. Goods that are not scarce, such as country air to a farmer, are not of economic interest because they do not figure in hard decisions. The farmer can have as much air as he wants without giving up anything else he values. Of course some scarce goods are scarcer than others. The scarcer a good the more of something you have to give up in order to obtain some of the good. Prices are often used to measure the relative scarcity of goods; however, the relationship between price and relative scarcity is a complex one.

Positive Economics and Normative Economics

In order to make a decision three kinds of information are needed: (1) a knowledge of the range of alternatives open to the decision maker; (2) a knowledge of the consequences of choosing each of the alternatives; and (3) a criterion that tells the decision maker which of the sets of consequences is most valuable to him. An example which we will deal with at length in Chapter 6 can serve to illustrate the role of each. A businessman is trying to decide how much of a good to produce. His range of alternatives then consists of each of the possible amounts his factory is capable of producing. The consequences of choosing each alternative can be summarized by means of two numbers for each: the cost of producing that amount and the revenue which can be obtained from selling it. Suppose our businessman would like his profits to be as high as possible. This is his criterion; therefore, he searches the alternatives for the one which provides the greatest difference between revenue and cost, and decides to execute this alternative.

The example also shows how price can be used to simplify decisions. The businessman was able to summarize the complex activity of producing and selling a good by means of the money cost of production and the money revenue from selling. Each of these numbers was derived in part from the prices of the goods used as inputs by the businessman and the price of the goods he produces. He is likely to use profits as a criterion because by obtaining more profits he increases his command over the goods and services which are sold at a price. Thus the existence of prices enables the businessman to make a complicated decision with relative ease, by using the prices to measure the value to him of the various available "compromises" (in which higher revenue requires higher cost).

Our example can serve to illustrate one of the major pitfalls of economic analysis—the failure to distinguish between what people do in practice and what they ought to do. Decisions involve values in a fundamental way: values provide the criterion by which alternatives are judged by the decision maker. Suppose that businessmen actually use the criterion of profit maximization in their decisions. This then is a fact of nature, a property of the real world. Positive economics studies the decision criteria that businessmen actually use in practice.

But ought businessmen to use that criterion? This is a different kind of question from the factual question: What criterion do businessmen actually use? By asking the "ought" question we are evaluating rather than describing. Naturally the answer depends on what set of values is being brought to bear on the problem. The owner of a business may ask this question with a view to the welfare of himself and his family. He wants to know which criterion to apply in running his own business if he is to make the decision which will be best from the point of view of his family interests. A congressman may ask the question with the public interest in mind. He is wondering if the public interest would be better served if businessmen were encouraged or compelled to use some other criterion. A union leader may answer this question with still another criterion in view. In normative economics we study such questions as what criterion businessmen ought to use.

Quite conceivably each of the above people will come to a different answer to the question as to what criterion businessmen ought to use, and perhaps none of them will conclude that profit maximization is the right one—even though, according to our assumption, this is in fact what businessmen do. But disagreement as to what ought to be the case does not, in itself, change the facts. All too often in economics, arguments that appear to be concerned with the facts turn out to be concerned with the choice of values by the protagonists. Since we must describe values in order to describe decisions, it is important to try to keep our own values out of the picture during this stage. But since we are concerned that the economy work well we must eventually bring in our values if we are to choose the right economic policies. This brings the danger of confusion perilously close and requires constant vigilance to avoid the mixing of description and evaluation.

Because economics is a social science and because facts and values are so closely intertwined in decision making, the danger of fallacious argument is especially great. Advocates of a particular policy have a tendency to ignore or misstate factors which weaken their position. Only by a careful reading combined with some prior knowledge can the flaws in this kind of argument be exposed. Arguments may be subject to four kinds of failures:

1. *A failure of logic.* Most arguments offered by economists are not internally inconsistent in the sense that you can prove proposition A to be *both* true and false from the given assumptions. The most common failing is the non sequitur, in which it is asserted that a proposition follows from the given assumptions when in fact it does not. And among non sequiturs the most famous and probably most common in economics is the fallacy of composition, in which one states that what is true of the part must also be true of the whole. For example, a businessman or labor leader may argue that imposing a tariff on the imports of product X will benefit the country by protecting the economy from low priced foreign competition. It is probably true that the tariff will protect industry X in this way, but the higher price for the product that results will hurt many consumers. The effect on the economy as a whole is far from clear.

Economic Arguments

5

2. *Factual error.* Many propositions about economic phenomena are debatable in the sense that available evidence does not permit a firm judgment as to their truth or falsity. For example, representatives of industry and of consumer groups may differ over the amount by which domestic prices will rise when the tariff on X is imposed. Though careful study may serve to narrow the range of such differences, it is rare indeed that they can be eliminated. However, there are a number of propositions about which there is a considerable measure of agreement among economists. Often they deal with the direction of change of some variable; less frequently with the magnitude of change.

► *Most economic propositions are based on the important ceteris paribus ("other things equal") condition, which says that the particular proposition is generally true only if all other relevant aspects of the economic situation remain unchanged.*

Even the best of economic propositions may appear to be falsified because other things *were* changing and swamped the effects of the given causal pattern. For example, the law of diminishing marginal returns states that increasing the use of one input to a production process while holding the other inputs constant will lead eventually to a steady decline in the additional output obtained. One might think that this proposition could be applied directly to agriculture in the United States. The government limits the amount of land that farmers can plant in several basic crops such as corn. Diminishing returns would seem to imply, *ceteris paribus,* that as more seed is added to this fixed amount of land, the increase in yield of corn would become less and less. The increases that have occurred over the years do not show this, however. The reason of course is that other things were not equal. For one thing, there were also increasing amounts of fertilizer applied to the land. For another, technological change, especially the development of new kinds of seed, has been quite revolutionary. These facts do not prove that diminishing returns is wrong as a proposition about the economy; only that it is not relevant to this particular situation. Clearly successful application of the scientific parts of economics is not a simple business.

3. *Nonoptimality.* The problem here is that the writer has failed to perceive that there is another alternative which will serve his own ends more effectively than the alternative he is advocating. An economic planner in an underdeveloped country, say, takes as his goal to maximize the rate of growth of national product. He advocates the building of a steel mill to help achieve this end. But being city bred he does not realize that the foreign exchange needed to buy

and import equipment for the steel mill would yield even more input if devoted to importing tractors, seeds, and technical experts to help farmers increase their productivity.

4. *The wrong choice of goals.* Here the advocate may have favored eliminating poverty as rapidly as possible as his criterion for choosing among alternatives, when instead he should have chosen the goal of maximizing the freedom of the citizenry. How can one argue that he "should" have chosen a different goal? One reason is that the reader's fundamental moral values may differ from the advocate's. In this case the disagreement is too fundamental for economics to be of any help in reconciling the opponents. It may well be that no reconciliation is possible. But more often economists can usefully engage in debate over the question of goals or values, because few of us are able to specify, in a way that is a practical guide to action, just what our fundamental goals are. At the practical level, most statements of goals are derivative—are in fact partly policy statements which not only say what is good but also say something about how to achieve this happy condition. For example does someone who wants a maximum of freedom always oppose any extension of government intervention in the economy? Does having as a goal the highest possible standard of living for the populace determine what proportion of resources ought to go into investment in any one year?

As a consequence of the derivative nature of most statements of goals, economists may discuss their implications in the hope that the means and ends may be further separated and that after this has been done agreement can be reached on both means and some more fundamental set of ends. In controversy economists who are not merely trying to score debating points are often engaged in this attempt to untangle values, debatable facts, and "undoubted truths." Skill in this undertaking is the real hallmark of intellectual maturity in our discipline.

2

Who Makes the Decisions?

Everyone in the United States makes a considerable number of decisions every day, quite a large fraction of which deal with economic problems. However, the United States, like all societies, is highly organized. From the point of view of decision making, organization imposes patterns on this vast horde of decisions. Groups of people become closely associated and their decisions become coordinated and interdependent. Because many of these groups are quite stable, the patterns of behavior that emerge persist over considerable periods of time.

This feature suggests a way of simplifying the picture of economic decision making. Instead of dealing with the decisions of each individual in a society we may deal with the economic decisions that emerge from these groups. In many cases we may even treat the group as if it were a single individual, speaking of the group's decision. Thus we have the concept of the decision unit.

▶ *An economic decision unit is a collection of individuals who are so closely associated in the making of a range of economic decisions that, over this range, their decisions can be consolidated and treated as if they were made by a single individual.*

The family may serve to illustrate the implications of this approach, which is made throughout economic analysis. A family contains several people, one or more of whom usually contribute income to the household by their work. Some expenditures are made by family members independently, some are the product of joint consultation and decision. Disagreements may arise and may lead to heated discussions over the proper decisions to make. All this is is ignored by our consolidated treatment of the family as a decision unit. Only the results of the discussions are of interest and we rely on the fact that the family is typically a highly cohesive social unit so that in general there is a rough consensus among influential members of a family as to major economic decisions. Indeed by definition the family persists as a decision unit only so long as consensual decision making about economic matters predominates. Of course families do split into separate decision units from time to time. When a child grows up, gets a job, and lives away from home he acquires a large measure of independence and properly becomes a new decision unit in his own right. And marriage is the merger of all or part of two decision units.

A key feature common to all households in a market economy is the budget. Each household has a flow of income from various goods and services it provides to others, including saving. Our analysis of household decisions centers around the budget, which serves as a sort of clearing house for its economic decisions. Since incomes and expenditures are flows, we usually measure them in terms of dollars per month or per year: a house rents for $100 per month, or one's income is $8,000 per year. It is because most household decisions in a market economy require the making of deals involving either the receipt or payment of money that the budget becomes such a useful center of attention for analysis. The budget serves to ration economic decisions, showing which ones are feasible and how much in the way of unchosen alternatives must be sacrificed if any given alternative is to be chosen.

In the mid-1960s the United States contained about 45 million families having two or more members, with an additional 10 million individuals living alone or with friends, or a total of some 55 million households. In contrast to the situation a hundred years ago, most families contained only two generations, parents and children, with grandparents living separately. Family size had declined, too; only 10 per cent of the families had four or more children. The median family contained one child (half the families lie on the one-or-fewer-children side, half on the one-or-more-children side of the median), and had an income of about $7,000 to spend in a year.

Households—that is, families and separate individuals—are obviously a quite diverse group, containing Rockefellers, lawyers, shop-keepers, metalworkers, and the unemployed and their families. In terms of education, income, training, attitudes, and experience the variety has if anything expanded over the years as the United States has become richer and more complex. It would indeed be futile to seek very precise answers to questions about the behavior of house-holds in terms of averages. However, for many purposes there are enough similarities among them to make the analysis of the house-hold in general a topic worthy of study. Economists have developed a method of analysis of household behavior which brings out sys-tematically important features which households have in common and many of the ways in which they differ. This analysis will be the subject of Chapter 4.

Businesses ▶ *A business is a decision unit which takes the making of profit as a major goal.*

The distinction between household and business is often not very sharp. A family that is moving may try to sell some of its effects right in the house. A dressmaker may work at home and intersperse house-keeping with sewing. A handyman or a writer may operate from his home and not make a clear distinction between his business and family activities and income. Of the nearly five million American businesses, well over three million are proprietorships, in which there is a single owner whose income is treated essentially as family in-come for tax purposes. Closely related to the proprietorships are partnerships, which are a sort of merger of families for business purposes.

However, most business in the United States is carried out by a quite distinctive form of organization, the corporation. There are fewer than 700,000 corporations in the United States and they, too, vary widely in size, with assets ranging from the insignificant up to the nearly $34 billion of American Telephone and Telegraph. The largest two hundred of these do perhaps a quarter or more of the nation's private business.

Corporations are established by obtaining a charter from a govern-ment, generally a state. The laws and forms of corporate organization and formation vary widely. However, private business corporations have a few features in common:

1. They are legal persons. The corporation can sue or be sued as if it were an individual. As a consequence of this it can, through the agency of its management, make decisions, write checks, order goods, and otherwise act as a responsible individual in the conduct of busi-ness. This is really the central feature of the corporate form of or-ganization, from which stem most of its advantages.

2. Being a legal person conveys immortality. As long as there are net assets and a management, and the charter is in order, a corporation may exist indefinitely. This can save a great deal of cost and confusion as compared, say, to the partnership, where the withdrawal of a partner from the concern for any reason usually means the formal dissolution of the concern. Even in the sole (single-owner) proprietorship the absence of an established procedure for orderly succession from one owner to the next can on occasion cause trouble. The corporation itself does not have to face this difficulty, though of course struggle for control of a corporation can have a similar effect.

3. Because of the limited liability of stockholders capital is relatively easy to obtain. In a proprietorship or partnership each owner is liable for the debts of the organization up to the full extent of his own assets. The dangers of being a victim of fraud or mismanagement by a partner or manager are thus very great. A corporation, however, accumulates capital by selling stock, or, roughly speaking, certificates of partial ownership. The liability of the stockholder for the debts of the corporation is limited to the amount of his investment in the corporation. A man who became a partner in twenty partnerships would probably be running a very great risk of ruin if the organizations were large and if for each of the firms there was some likelihood of failure. But a man who owns stock in twenty large corporations is probably being prudent by spreading his risks of loss widely and thereby substantially reducing his own risk of ruin. This feature of corporations accounts for the very large size they can attain. Large proprietorships are something of a rarity.

4. Corporations are managed by the board of directors, who are elected by the stockholders, and by the executive officers appointed by the board. Contrary to popular opinion, the primary legal obligation of these managing officers is not to the stockholders but to the corporation itself. This corporation, being inanimate, cannot defend itself properly, so the officers and the board are required by law to act in good faith as defenders of the interests of the corporation. The question of how and in whose interests decisions are made in practice will be taken up later. However, it is clear that making profits is a central aim of private business corporations, whatever type of management they possess.

5. As a corporation grows its value increases—that is, its owners can sell it for more money on the market. The market price of the stock, or certificates of ownership, which the corporation has issued measures this value. A corporation may sell additional certificates of ownership on the market as a means of financing growth. In addition to various kinds of stock certificates corporations also sell bonds to the public. These are simply debts; the corporation borrows the

sum of money named on the face of the bond and agrees to pay back the principal with interest after some fixed term of years. Bonds differ from personal loans made at the bank or from a finance company only in that there is a regular market for many types of bonds. That is, the right to be a creditor of a corporation in some amount can usually be bought and sold much more easily than the right to be the creditor of an individual, for obvious reasons. Otherwise the bondholder's status is like that of any creditor. The corporation is obliged to make good its obligations to creditors before paying out dividends to stockholders, since the latter are part owners and therefore are more deeply participants in the successes and failures of the corporation. The markets in which stocks and bonds are traded are very complex because there is a tremendous variety of terms on which any corporation can issue securities. The interest rate or yield of the bonds and the term (the length of time before the debt is to be repaid) can vary, as can the order in which profits are paid out to the various types of stockholders. Many stocks are nonvoting, which means that the holders do not have the right to participate in stockholders' meetings at which, among other things, the board of directors is elected. Ownership participation, risk, yield, and term are some of the principal ways in which securities may differ from one another.

6. Corporations, like households, have budgets. Because productive activity plays such an important role in economic life, we will spend a good deal of time analyzing the economic decisions of firms, beginning in Chapter 6. The problems are very like those faced by a household, though of course for large organizations a great many more budgetary decisions must be made and specialization and division of labor in the making of these decisions is often carried to great lengths. Nevertheless, as was noted in Chapter 1, there is a certain fundamental simplicity in the problem faced by a business which is interested in making as high a level of profits as possible. The simplicity stems from the fact that money and prices are the elements by which alternatives may be compared. The decision whether a line of goods should be continued can easily be made once the money costs of the alternatives have been calculated and compared with the revenues which each will produce. The greatest profits lie with the alternative in which there is the greatest difference between cost and revenue. Of course, it may not be easy to estimate costs and revenue; still, the profit calculation of the firm is far more firmly based in measurable reality than is the attempt of a household to maximize its satisfaction.

Government   No one can doubt that American government is big and growing bigger. Both taxes and spending have been moving pretty steadily upward since early in the century. The question is whether it has become too big or is still not big enough.

In one recent cartoon two preachers are discussing affairs of their church. One says to the other: "Our main problem is that the government keeps outpromising us." In another, a group of senators, including Senator Goldwater, are seated around a table and engaged in heated discussion. One of them is saying: "But Barry, the government has *always* run the Post Office." These two cartoons with the appeal on the one hand to questions of political tactics and on the other to tradition are perhaps typical of the approach to the question of the proper role of government in popular discussion.

Appeals of this kind are likely to interest economists as well as others. However, in his professional capacity the economist seeks to find some more fundamental criterion for judging the appropriate functions of government. For an economist living in a market economy a criterion is immediately suggested: let government perform those economic services which cannot be performed efficiently by private interests operating through a market. The next step would be to ask: What are the properties of a good or service which determine whether or not the market can provide it efficiently?

Before turning to this question, we should give more attention to an evaluation of the plausibility of the market criterion. Hundreds of millions of people live in economies today where the government performs many of the functions which markets mediate in the United States. For them our criterion might seem rather peculiar, so we had better try to clarify the issue.

Freedom, Welfare, and the Market Mechanism

Those who object to a large and increasing role for government argue that it is a threat to freedom. However, freedom is not a word with a single simple meaning, as can be seen from the fact that those who advocate *more* government also often defend their policies as generating more freedom. Perhaps the first step in interpreting the government's role in terms of things the market cannot do is to explicate the various meanings of freedom.

In a recent thorough survey of the idea of freedom through the ages it was suggested that definitions fall generally into three types: (1) those that relate freedom to the range of choices; (2) those that relate it to the personality traits of a particular type of man; and (3) those that relate it to the process of self-realization of the individual in society.[2]

It is important to note that the freedom with which we are con-

2. Mortimer Adler, *The Idea of Freedom* (New York: Doubleday, 1958), vol. 1, p. 26.

cerned has to do with human interaction, not with man's relation to nature or to God. As someone has put it: "Not determinism but coercion is the opposite of freedom." We will examine the relevance of each of these three definitions bearing this limitation in mind.

The range of choice criterion is the one that fits most easily the framework of analysis of the economist. Freedom in this sense is closely associated with the operation of markets. Consider the individual who comes into the marketplace. He has a stock of goods and money. He finds himself exposed to a variety of proposals for trading and may himself initiate such proposals. If the market functions well, so that he has sufficient information about possible deals, he is able to find the maximum possible satisfaction subject only to the constraints of his own resources and the restriction that he must not make others worse off. The first constraint depends on the initial distribution of wealth. The second, however, is guaranteed by the market mechanism itself. Everyone is free not to trade, so only those trades which will make both parties to the deal better off will be consummated. Thus in a sense the market maximizes freedom; for each participant it provides the maximum range of alternatives consistent with the above two conditions.

It has been argued that the market need not provide a good outcome. This qualification does not conflict with our present argument, for it is not being claimed that the results of freedom will necessarily be good. In fact they may be extremely bad. The very poor may starve because they can make no deals that provide them with enough food; their freedom is subject to this rather stringent constraint. But given the initial distribution of wealth the market does not reduce their freedom, and should increase it, if this can be done within the two constraints.

It was not necessary to say anything about personality in discussing range-of-choice freedom, though at the very least we are assuming that individuals are capable of independent action. But many writers have felt that a free society must be a society of free men, which means that their attitudes and behavior must be of certain kinds if freedom is to be preserved. Independence of mind and spirit is one rather obvious property associated with free men. It provides for some basis other than conformity or obedience for determining one's course of action. Another likely property is curiosity, or active seeking to fulfill one's independently determined goals.

The market would seem to be a place where independence could be preserved successfully and where search behavior would prosper. In a market a person can provide himself with any combination of goods, labor, and leisure he wishes, constrained not by specific taboos or social pressures but only by his income and talent. He has less to fear from others because they cannot compel him to act, but can only bargain with him. Because the market economy is a complex one, he may fall short of his goals unless he spends a significant fraction of his time in searching out ways to improve his position. So it appears that the market can play an important assisting role in promoting both of the first two kinds of freedom.

Freedom of self-realization is a broader and vaguer and perhaps deeper concept of freedom than the other two. It is partly a matter of range of choice, for an individual must have appropriate opportunities if he is to realize himself. It is partly a matter of personality, for an individual must be capable of seeking and choosing those courses of action which will promote self-realization. In addition, it is partly a matter of dynamics, of movement over time, for self-realization is presumably rather like the gradual development and opening of a flower bud. This in turn implies that both personality and environment must be changing in appropriate ways.

It is rather difficult to say anything about the relation between a concept so all-embracing as this and the operation of markets. At most, one can point to the flexibility of the market system. Its responses to changing opportunities will be very rapid, provided there are people actively seeking out these opportunities, and provided that the market system permits the generating and transmission of information about them. Opportunity for self-realization is a striking and fundamental conception of freedom, but its very generality makes it difficult to associate this kind of freedom with specific institutional arrangements.

Yet another slogan about freedom: in essence it consists in replacing brutality with sensibility. This may seem quite similar to the idea that restricting coercion increases freedom. However, there is an important distinction, one which appears to change the nature of freedom rather substantially. This is the appeal to empathy or fellow-feeling contained in the word "sensibility." Here the process of increasing freedom consists in the development of the ability of members of society to understand the desires and actions of others, and, of course, to act on this growing understanding.

This notion is quite different from the ones we discussed earlier, and, I think, comes much closer to the idea of welfare as a criterion for social action. People interested in promoting the welfare of society are interested in promoting the well-being of the members of society. This requires understanding plus a willingness to act on the basis of understanding.

It is often claimed that a welfare orientation is inconsistent with successful operation of the market, since it is self-interested individuals who are the primary actors in the market place. As will be seen

15

in the next section, it is probably true that the range-of-choice kind of freedom is threatened by a welfare orientation among market participants. It may well be true that welfare orientation also reduces the incentive to search for marketable types of opportunities. To the extent that this is true one may be faced with a hard choice in deciding whether or not to expand or curtail the range of the action of the market mechanism. That is, it may be that whichever way one goes a price must be paid, in one direction in terms of freedom, in the other in terms of welfare.

On Determining the Economic Role for Government

It has been argued that there is a close association, at least in principle, between freedom, defined in some commonly used ways, and the operation of a market economy. This connection suggests the criterion for the role of government in economic decision-making which was mentioned earlier: use the government only when the market fails. After looking at the ways in which the market can fail to do a good job, we will return to the implications of welfare as a criterion for determining the respective roles of private market and government.

Paternalism is one reason for intervening in the market. For example, children and the physically and mentally disabled are not thrown into the marketplace to see what their services will bring. Closely related to paternalism is the restriction on sale of narcotics. In these situations society steps in to impose behavior on certain members or on some of the behavior of all members. Implicit in such acts is the assertion that some people know best what is best for others. Since the market does not permit such impositions, some other type of social interaction must be resorted to.

A second reason for intervention in the market is monopoly. A monopoly occurs when a single participant acquires all of some scarce good or service. There are famous stories, mostly from the nineteenth century, of attempts to corner, or monopolize, markets in everything from matches to gold. Monopolists are in a strong position to make large profits from raising the price of their product. However, the ability of the monopolist to do this varies widely with the product. If there are close substitutes, the monopolist cannot raise prices very much or his customers will all shift to another product. In a sense there are a great many monopolies in the United States. The American Tobacco Company has a monopoly of Lucky Strikes, for example. But substitutes like Camels and even filtered Kents are so close that we generally think of the product as being cigarettes, a product in which the American Tobacco Company does not have a monopoly.

Because of their production technology, some monopolies cannot be broken up into several smaller producers without paying a price in efficiency. These are called "natural" or "technical" monopolies. The provision of telephone service is an example. For monopolies of this kind one possible form of state intervention—breaking the monopoly up into a number of competing firms—is less desirable than in other cases. Monopolies can restrict range-of-choice freedom in comparison with a more competitive form of market organization. As will be seen later, this is by no means certain, and when there is an efficiency cost to be paid in the latter case there may be no reason for opposing monopoly. Of course, there are several ways to administer monopolies—for example, by leaving them alone, by regulating them, or by nationalizing them. These alternatives, too, must be discussed later.

The third reason for intervention in the market occurs when there are external effects. External effects occur when third parties are affected by deals, which can happen in connection with both production and consumption. A factory may produce noxious smoke or smog as a by-product. People who live in the vicinity are affected, though they played no part in the decisions which led the factory to go into production. Pleasant effects may also result from production, as when a farmer's increased plantings of apple trees create more nectar-laden blossoms to the unintended benefit of a neighboring beekeeper. An example from consumption would be the effect on an envious person when his neighbor turns in his Chevrolet for a new Cadillac. The same event would have a positive, but still external, effect on a sympathetic neighbor.

The common feature of all these examples is that satisfaction or dissatisfaction is created for individuals who played no role in the market agreements that generated the effects. The welfare of third parties is thus increased or decreased in a way that offers them no choice. In the case of pleasant or satisfaction-generating by-products, freedom is not restricted by the acts, and the market does not give ideal results. An ideal solution can be attained only if all the affected individuals are party to the decision.

One type of good which seems especially suited to being provided outside the market is the collective good.

► *A collective good is indivisible in the sense that if some people consume the good then the good is available to others, whether they wish to consume it or not.*

There are no market rules for a collective good which will determine how the good is to be allocated among participants. The individual household does not have the independent option to buy and consume the good or not. Nor can the individual household independently influence the level of production of the good. Such is the case with defense expenditures. An increase in defense expenditures provides (roughly) an increase in the service "defense" to all members of society. Of course, individuals will differ as to how much defense they want, but the amount they get cannot be varied to fit their differing wants. Many of the services provided traditionally by government, such as police and fire protection, have at least to some extent this property of being collective goods.

Whenever paternalism seems appropriate, or external effects or monopoly are present, the market will tend to restrict the freedom of some of the participants in comparison with conceivable alternatives. This in itself is insufficient reason for turning over to the state control of all such situations, for there is another alternative: the voluntary association. In the United States most paternalistic activity with respect to children comes from a particular form of voluntary association, the family.[3] Some of the rest is provided by charitable organizations, while the state provides the remainder, both in the form of institutional care and legal restraints on the exercise of paternalism by parents. To some extent trade associations in industry provide general information to firms which is useful but which it might not pay the individual firm to collect. Trade associations, which are typically supported by groups of firms producing similar products, are attempting to realize some of these external effects through voluntary association. They may also be trying to form a monopoly, but that is another story.

However, voluntary associations are not likely to be useful in eliminating the harmful effects of monopoly, and frequently they are ineffective in dealing with the other types of market failure. For example, volunteer fire departments have operated successfully where, among other things, community feeling was strong. However in large cities they have proven ineffective. Part of the problem has been that citizens who received the protection too often were unwilling to contribute voluntarily to the support of the organization, while the fire department itself could hardly refuse to serve noncontributors. Under these circumstances effective fire protection can be provided only when contributions are made compulsory, which requires the force of law.

An anarchist who values freedom above all things would probably refuse to accept any form of compulsion. A liberal, however, is likely to claim that the exercise of compulsion in the interest of bet-

3. Actually the state imposes a variety of constraints on the family which restrict the scope of voluntary acion. This qualificaion applies to most voluntary associations in modern industrial societies.

ter service may be justified on the ground that freedom is not really the issue. For the individual's range of choice is restricted in any case. For example, he must either take elaborate and costly precautions against fire entirely on his own, or accept the low-grade service which a poorly supported volunteer service will provide, or accept compulsory taxation together with good service. It is not clear that individuals are freer in one of these situations than in the others, in terms of any of our three definitions of freedom.

In applying the criterion of freedom in judging market situations, it is often argued that the use of government should always be feared since it always entails compulsion through legislation. That is, it is claimed that one should be prepared to accept some cost in terms of efficient outcomes in order to avoid this compulsion. This argument seems to imply that some other criterion than freedom is being used to decide between government and market, for otherwise one would be prepared to accept *any* cost in order to avoid *any* reduction in freedom. For most people it is doubtless necessary to have an additional criterion in order to deal with those cases in which the freedom criterion does not give a decision, as in the fire-protection case, where changing from one solution to another has the effect of increasing freedom for some and decreasing it for others. Welfare is probably the criterion added by most people.

If one were motivated solely by the welfare criterion, one would make a great many decisions in the same way as if freedom were the criterion. Where paternalism, external effects, or monopoly are present, welfare too provides a reason for intervening in the market. However, the welfare criterion probably takes one farther toward nonmarket solutions. For example, take the problem of low-income families. Where individuals have been rendered incapable of caring for themselves by misfortune, both criteria might well call for government intervention to help out. In the case of those in temporary difficulties where lives were not at stake, however, the freedom criterion might well call for opposing intervention on the grounds that by rewarding inertia or passivity the free personality of the recipients was being weakened. Application of the welfare criterion, on the other hand, might lead to the argument that there is a large element of chance in the operation of the market mechanism. Bad luck rather than lack of energy, skill, or foresight is involved in many failures. To be sure, the more energetic will find their way out of these temporary setbacks, but their recovery does not change the fact that families may suffer greatly during the process. If one is understanding and sympathetic, it will be hard to refuse help even if in some fraction of the cases we are rewarding indolence.

The principles on which our political tradition was founded and which are supported by liberals and conservatives alike in both major political parties today seem to contain welfare as well as freedom. The difference among participants is not a matter of whether we should believe in one or the other exclusively, but in their relative importance. Whatever mixture we may choose individually, it seems clear that information as to the extent to which paternalism, external effects, or monopoly may be present will be pertinent to our decisions as to whether market or government is the appropriate organizational form in any given area of the economy. In fact we will be returning to these two criteria of freedom and welfare whenever a question of economic policy arises.

Government Criteria

So far we have been talking about what the government ought to do. But what in fact is the criterion by which government decisions are made? Clearly governments are not profit maximizers. They are supposed to serve the public interest but, as we have seen, there is much disagreement as to just what the public interest is. Legislatures reflect a variety of interest group pressures as well as the ideals and aspirations of citizens and legislators. In the United States there is not only the Federal government but also fifty state governments and thousands of local governments, each with some measure of independence in making economic decisions. Since there is no generally accepted theory of government behavior, there is not much economic analysis of governments as economic decision units. But government cannot be ignored; and in the final chapter of this book we will consider a few aspects of government decision making.

In summary, freedom and welfare are probably the chief criteria used by Americans to evaluate economic alternatives. Decision making by means of markets very often serves both criteria, increasing simultaneously material welfare and the opportunities open to participants, as well as encouraging independent behavior. However, in many cases the use of markets or of voluntary decision processes poses hard decisions. Typically these hard decisions arise because of the government's ability to intervene in the market process. The hard choice may be between freedom and welfare: whether to have more welfare and less freedom, or the reverse. Often too the hard choice is a matter of *freedom for whom*, or *welfare for whom*—that is, choosing one alternative rather than another increases the welfare or freedom of one group at the expense of another. On issues of this kind men and even governments are divided; hence the difficulty in specifying a single decision criterion for government.

3

Markets

Markets have been with us during most of our recorded history. Traders have left their traces in cuneiform tablets from the time of Nebuchadnezzar, and there are hints of long-distance trading across Europe thousands of years before that. Crassus made his fortune dealing in ancient Roman real estate. Towns and cities rose in medieval France, prospering from the market fairs which became annual events of the towns, attracting merchants and producers from near and far. In early modern times merchants made fortunes by loaning money to kings on the security of such royal properties as mines.

But all the varied forms of early markets pale beside the number, size, and variety of markets today. On a fairly slow day some five million shares of stock will change hands on the New York Stock Exchange. A small underdeveloped country may produce over 100,000 different products. And the goods may be exchanged in an infinite variety of ways, from the haggling of the bazaar to the take-it-or-leave-it prices fixed by the government, from the direct confrontation of producer and consumer at the cobbler's to the telegraphic agreements of bond brokers acting for middlemen, from the buying of strawberries to be consumed this evening to the placing of orders for supersonic jets to be delivered seven years hence.

Of course, markets are not the only way in which goods are provided by producers to consumers. The simplest economy of all would be one in which producer and consumer were always the same person so that no trading was necessary. This is a rare situation, however, though the Shoshone Indians, who lived on acorns and small game in the Great Basin of the American West during the nineteenth century, came pretty close. Another way is to have some authority collect and distribute the economy's output according to rules of their own making. The temple civilizations of ancient Egypt and the Near East used a mixture of both these systems, and market trading as well. In the contemporary world a rather similar procedure helps to provide military security for a nation. Some countries provide medical services on this basis, though the producers of medical services are paid and may have some influence over prices. As these examples suggest, there are many variations and mixtures of market types and controls which lie between the two extremes of no external intervention and no freedom of choice for the participants. Yet another intermediate stage occurs in the Soviet Union for most consumer goods. These are produced in number and kind according to a plan laid down by the state. They are then sold to consumers on markets in which the prices have also been set by the state.

Markets are overwhelmingly important for the United States where they play some role in the provision of over 90 per cent of the goods produced. Even in highly centralized economies like the Soviet Union and Communist China there is some role for markets. For this reason alone the analysis of markets should lie at the heart of economics. But there is more to it than this. It turns out that market analysis is also of great usefulness in analyzing and understanding other ways of providing goods and services to a community.

It would be tedious indeed to look at each of the possible varieties of markets in turn and see how they work. It would also be confusing, for it would tend to conceal from view some fundamental similarities in the ways all markets work. Instead we will begin with a highly simplified description of a market, one which will have some relevance for all markets. Then the process of differentiating markets can proceed systematically in terms of the impact of various kinds of differences on our model market.

Market Supply and Demand

What is a market? This is not an easy question to answer. From the examples given above it is clear that a market need not be a fixed place, nor involve the trading of a single good, nor even involve a physical act of exchange. The defining characteristics of the market come not from the place or time or kind of good involved but from the kind of behavior of the participants.

The basic element of market behavior is the *deal*. A deal is an agreement for the exchange of goods and services and so must involve at least two parties. But some deals fall through and yet are important in determining the way a market works. Hence they must be included. We may call a potential deal any specific offer to make a deal, whether or not there is a taker.

▶   *A market, then, is a collection of deals, actual and potential.*

To a considerable extent the particular collection of deals that is called a market is determined as a matter of convenience. For example, if a grocery chain is thinking of putting up a new store in a suburb, the company's market analysts will be interested in the size of the market (including potential as well as actual deals) for groceries in the neighborhood of the site. Farmers and bakers and military procurement officers all over the country may be interested in the market for wheat whose communications center is the "pit" of the Chicago commodity exchange. Stockholders all over the world are interested in the stock market in which thousands of different commodities—stock certificates—are traded in a variety of communications centers, of which the New York Stock Exchange is only one. Peasants in an isolated Greek village are interested in the market for their grapes for which a single middleman may be the only potential purchaser. Deals for the same commodity, say steel I-beams, may be thought of as constituting a single market, or as a small part of the market for steel; and deals for steel may be thought of as comprising a regional, a national, or even an international market.

We may choose any way of combining deals into markets that seems useful for our purposes. Of course, a price is paid when we combine trading in many goods into a single market for analytical purposes. In doing so, we lose a good deal of information related to the specific properties of the less inclusive markets and the interactions among them. The choice of scope must be determined by the use to which the analysis is to be put.

One other simplification: Let us suppose that our good, which we may as well call X, is always bought and sold for money. Barter is inconvenient because it complicates the problem of making deals. Owners of X who want Y must find someone who both wants X and has some Y he is willing to trade. If there is something available that everybody values, like money, the operation of trading X for Y can be broken into two deals, each of which is made in a different market. So the market for X is one in which deals are made which involve only X and money.

What determines the potential deals that are available in the market during any period of time? One factor, obviously, is the usefulness of the good. To some extent this is a matter of taste; many people will ignore the eggplant market completely. But human nature as well as nature itself provides some similarities in tastes; there are few who ignore the market for grain products entirely. The stock of X that participants have, of course, determines whether they will be buyers or sellers as well as the size of the deals they will offer. Another factor is the price of other goods. This can act in two ways. On the one hand, the price of related goods affects the willingness to buy or sell X. The price of cigars has an effect on the amount of cigarettes buyers will want. And the price of labor has an effect on the amount of cigarettes producers are willing to sell at a given price. The second way other prices act is indirect. The higher other prices are, the less income potential buyers will have available to buy X. Another way of saying this is that the incomes of potential buyers affect the amounts of the goods they are willing to buy.

A great many factors influence the amount and kind of potential deals offered on a market. We want to concentrate on the internal working of the market; so we will divide the factors into two kinds: the exogenous and the endogenous factors.

► *Exogenous factors are those which influence the market outcomes but are not much influenced by what goes on in this particular market.*

Incomes are a good example of this; the incomes of most individuals are not much affected by variations in the price of cheese, but the amount of cheese bought is fairly strongly influenced by incomes. Tastes are another example, since by and large they, too, do not shift much with changes in levels of activity in a particular market. The same is often true of the prices of other goods. In analyzing our model market we will assume that these exogenous factors have already been determined and that they remain unchanged. They are the *"ceteris paribus"* of our problems.

► *Endogenous factors are those which affect the market and are in turn affected by it.*

They are the factors to be explained by market analysis. They consist of the price of the good and the quantity traded. Obviously these are factors which are internal to the market since they are the most direct product of the deals.

In order to get a picture in diagram form of the operation of the market for X, we turn to the famous laws of supply and demand. We must now divide all potential deals involving X into two kinds: those in which deals are offered to sell X and those in which deals are offered to buy X. The former constitute the supply side of the market and the latter the demand side. The laws of supply and demand are explanations of how these two groups of potential deals are interwoven to determine the collection of actual deals and the endogenous factors, the quantities and prices at which X is exchanged.

The potential deals on the demand side of the market can be organized into a list, assuming for the moment that we know all about the participants in the market, their tastes, incomes, etc., and that all these exogenous factors remain unchanged regardless of the situation in the market for X. We then ask how much of X will participants offer deals to buy when the price is $10. We put the answer at the head of the list. The second row answers the same question when the price is $5, the third row when the price is $4, and so on. A hypothetical set of such data is provided in Table 3.1.

However, a more convenient way to show this information appears in Figure 3.1. The diagram presents the same information in a series

Table 3.1—Potential Deals to Buy X

Price	Quantity
10	2
5	4
4	7
3	10
2	14
1	20

Figure 3.1—Two ways to show demand for a good.

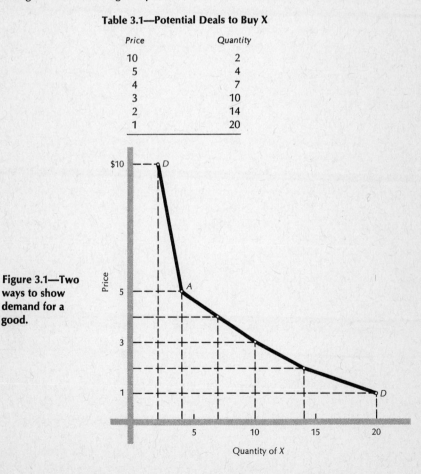

25

of points. Each point corresponds to a row of the table. By measuring horizontally from the vertical axis to the point we find the quantity, and by measuring vertically from the horizontal axis we find the price at which the quantity will be bought. Thus point A in the diagram corresponds to the second row in the table, telling us that at a price of $5 participants are prepared to buy a total of four units. Notice that each point on the diagram gives two bits of information: a price and a quantity.

Note that the list of potential deals to buy in Table 3.1 covers only a few possible prices. Since we are supposed to know all about the participants, there is no reason why we cannot make a much longer list, showing how the amount that would be bought varies with each small change in prices. To do this, say, for each nickel change in prices would make a very long list, but it would not necessarily make the diagram any longer. Indeed all we need do is draw a line through all the points that appear on the list. For such a small diagram this would no doubt appear to the naked eye as a continuous line. As a consequence the line DD in the diagram contains a good deal more information than does the table and organizes the information in a convenient way.[1]

Elasticity of Demand

The picture of demand provided by Figure 3.1 suggests that we can now consider such things as the steepness of the demand curve. Since line DD is very steep above point A, it might seem that people are somewhat indifferent as to price. However, steepness is not always good evidence for this conclusion. Suppose that on the diagram we are measuring the amount of X in pounds. If we now draw the demand curve by measuring the amount bought in ounces, DD will slope downward only one sixteenth as fast as it does in Figure 3.1. If steepness were our criterion, we would conclude from the new diagram that people were very sensitive to price in the purchases at prices above $5.

To avoid confusions of this kind another measure of steepness is used, one that does not vary when the units in which prices or quantities are measured change. This measure is called *price elasticity*.

▶   *Price elasticity of demand is the ratio of the percentage change in quantity to the percentage change in price at some point on the demand curve.*

Thus quantity offers increase from four to seven pounds, or by 75 per cent, when the price changes from $5 to $4 or by 20 per cent. The elasticity at a price of $4 is then 75/20 or 3.75. Notice that

---

1. Of course some of this additional information may be inaccurate. People may not be willing to buy 12 pounds at $2.50 as our interpolation implies. But at the moment we are omniscient by assumption.

if we changed the units to ounces the elasticity would not change. Each quantity sold would be multiplied by 16, but the percentage change from $4 \times 16 = 64$ to $7 \times 16 = 112$ is still 75 per cent.[2]

The concept of price elasticity has a great many uses in economics. Not only does it measure the responsiveness of potential buyers to price changes in a way that is independent of the units we use in measuring prices and quantities; it also provides a means of comparing the responsiveness of different goods to price changes. For example, economists have measured statistically the price elasticity for food in general and for apples in particular; they are, respectively, .6 and 1.1 in the area of the demand curves in which purchases are usually made in Great Britain. So the demand for food is less sensitive to price changes than the demand for apples. This seems reasonable enough. Food is an important part of the budget of most families and is indispensable. If food prices rise, most people will economize somewhat more on other purchases in order not to go hungry. To be more precise, the elasticity tells us that a 10 per cent increase in the price of food will reduce food consumption by only about 6 per cent. On the other hand, apples are not indispensable and there are other fruits that can be substituted for them if apples become more expensive. As a result a 10 per cent rise in the price of apples will lead to an 11 per cent reduction in the amount purchased.

To make the problem of classifying goods in terms of price sensitivity easier, economists usually take the elasticity of 1 as a dividing point. Goods whose elasticity is greater than unity are said to be in elastic demand, and those whose elasticity is less than one in inelastic demand. The demand for apples is elastic while food is in inelastic demand.

The elasticity of demand at any point on the demand curve tells us what will happen to the total revenue or income of sellers if price is changed. Figure 3.1 shows that, if the deals at $5 are all taken up by the potential sellers, they will receive $5 \times 4 = \$20$. If instead the deals at $4 are taken up, sellers will receive $4 \times 7 = \$28$. That is, revenue increases when price is reduced. This is always true when demand is elastic.

▶ *When demand is inelastic, a reduction in price will always lead to a reduction in revenue, an increase to an increase. Thus a knowledge of the price elasticity of demand for his*

2. This is a very crude way to calculate elasticity. Note that the definition related elasticity to a particular point on the diagram. However, our calculation procedure gives a measure of the average elasticity of the two points from which the changes in price and quantity are derived. If the actual elasticity at one point is quite different from that at the other our average elasticity may not be a good measure of either. There are better ways of calculating elasticity, but they are more complicated. For our purposes the crude measure will suffice.

product can be very useful information for a businessman to have.

Most of the things that were just said about demand curves also apply to the construction of supply curves. Again we make a list, this time considering all potential deals that involve the sale of some X. These can be listed in terms of the amounts that will be given up at each price. As with demand, the supply, too, can be more conveniently represented on a diagram, and a smooth curve drawn to represent the points that determine price-and-quantity pairs. So long as we measure price and quantity in the same units, we can put both curves on a single diagram, as is done in Figure 3.2, where DD is the demand curve and SS the supply curve.

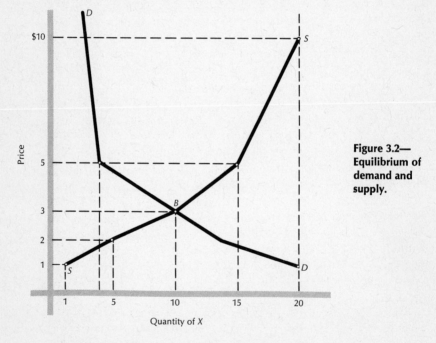

Figure 3.2—Equilibrium of demand and supply.

At point B in Figure 3.2 the two curves intersect. At this point the total amount people are willing to buy at the price of three dollars just equals the total amount people are willing to sell at that price. If the market can move to that point, everyone will be satisfied— that is, everyone who is willing to pay the price or to accept it will be able to make deals.

Of course, there is one obvious difference between our supply and demand curves: demand slopes downward to the right while supply slopes upward to the right. It seems reasonable enough that this should be so. When the price is lower, more people can afford more. When the price is higher more people are more willing to part with what they have and even try to produce more of it. There are occasional exceptions to this rule of slopes (see Chapter 4), but by and large the exceptions are of little practical importance.

One of the most interesting and important things about a market is that when it is functioning properly there are strong pressures forcing it to point B, which is called the equilibrium point.

▶ *The equilibrium point of a market is that price-and-quantity pair at which the amount supplied just equals the amount demanded.*

Suppose that for some reason the price of X is one dollar. The diagram shows that the amount people want at this price far exceeds the amount people are willing to part with. Many of those who want the good are willing to pay more for it; this we can see from the fact that even when the price is three times as high, more of X is demanded than will be supplied when the price is one dollar. It seems reasonable that rather than be left out these people will offer to pay a higher price for the good. All suppliers willing to sell the good at one dollar will be more than happy to sell it at two; indeed they will be willing to sell more than before and a few new sellers may also enter the market. At any rate, our supply curve tells us that one way or another four more units will be offered for sale at $2. So long as there is the pressure of excess demand over supply, the price will tend to rise.

The same sort of pressure develops when the price is higher than $2. Now potential sellers find that they have more goods on their hands than they want. If they are producers, they find their inventories of X building up alarmingly. To encourage more sales, they will tend to reduce their prices, and buyers will respond by increasing their purchases. As long as price remains above the equilibrium level, this pressure will persist.

A market that works this way is called stable because of its tendency to move toward a particular point whenever it is disturbed and to remain at this equilibrium point in the absence of disturbance. All markets for which our assumptions to date hold are stable; this means that the vast majority of markets in the economy are stable. However, there are some potentially unstable markets, as we will see later. Nevertheless, this fact of widespread stability should be reassuring to those living in a market economy.

Much of what has been said to this point about markets can now be summarized in a single sentence:

▶ ▶ *On most markets actual deals tend to be made at a single price.*

Up to now we have assumed that the exogenous factors, such as incomes and prices of other goods, have remained unchanged. However, in a time period of any length one would expect some changes to occur, and a good market analysis should be able to show how the changes affect market outcomes. Let us begin with demand. If incomes rise but nothing else changes some people will probably want more of X than they had before. If X is an expensive item, such as an automobile, a modest increase in income might not lead many families to increase the number of cars they own; however, it probably would induce some to buy a new car sooner than they otherwise would have. These remarks are true regardless of the current equilibrium price for X. In terms of our diagram this means that the demand curve shifts to the right (for example, from DD to D'D' in Figure 3.3) which implies that at every price there are at least a few more potential deals to buy.

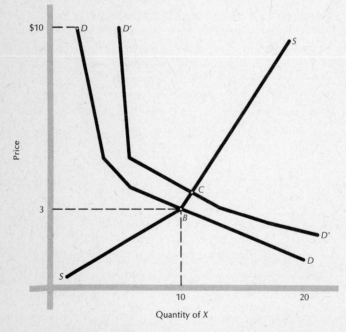

Figure 3.3—An increase in demand and a movement along the supply curve bring the market from one equilibrium point B to another C.

The same sort of effect is generated by other changes in the exogenous factors. If the price of a close substitute for X rises, the demand curve for X should shift to the right, because some people will be shifting to X from the other product. The same thing would happen if tastes changed for a number of people, so that they got relatively more enjoyment from consuming X than they did before.

When changes of this kind occur we say that *demand has increased*.

▶ *An increase in demand is a rightward shift in the demand schedule, which is caused by changes in exogenous factors which make the given commodity relatively more attractive than before.*

An increase in income, other things equal, will usually mean an increase in the demand for X. A fall in the price of X with no accompanying exogenous changes will lead to a *movement along* the demand curve. This movement results in an increase in the amount demanded. But by definition this is *not* an increase in demand. Of course, all this applies in reverse to reductions in income and to corresponding changes in the other exogenous factors. In all these cases the result is a decrease in demand, that is, a leftward shift in the demand curve.

Exogenous factors also operate on the supply curve. For example, a reduction in costs to producers of X may make them willing to sell more at any given price; hence the supply curve shifts to the right. Farm products are much affected by weather conditions, so that the supply surve for many such products may shift widely from one year to the next. Figure 3.4 shows a decrease in supply from SS to S'S'. This moves the equilibrium point from B to C, where fewer goods are sold at a higher price.

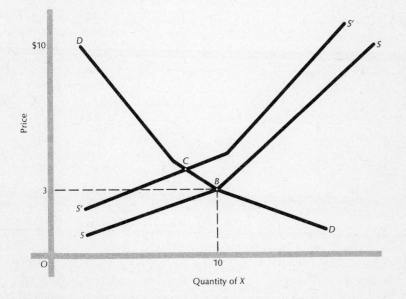

Figure 3.4—A movement along the demand curve and a decrease in supply bring the market from one equilibrium point B to another C.

**Freedom and
the Market
Economy**
A great deal of ink has been spilled over the question of whether
a market economy is the best way to promote human freedom. This
is a large and difficult subject, made much more difficult by the
vagueness and tendentiousness of many of the arguments. Of course
we cannot settle the issue, but already something can be said about it.

A market economy is an economy in which goods are moved from
one participant to another as the result of deals. It is an essential
element of a deal that each participant has the right to refuse to
accept the terms of any offer. If a deal is made, there is a strong
presumption that both parties are better off than before, since they
had the option of remaining in their original situation. There is thus
a strong voluntary element in the way in which markets operate
which supports the arguments of its defenders.

But this is not the whole story of the freedom-promoting qualities
of markets. The equilibrium point provides further support. When a
market is in equilibrium, it is true that there is no further deal, in
addition to the actual deals which are being consummated, that can
be found on the market which will make both parties to the deal
better off. The argument runs as follows: We assume that a person
is better off if he can buy the good at a lower price or can sell it at
a higher one. At the equilibrium point all who want the good at
the equilibrium price and all who are willing to sell at that price
have done so. So any further deals must take place at either a higher
price or a lower one. But no one is willing to pay a higher-than-
market price when he can get the good at a lower one, though
there are some who would be willing to sell a bit more X at that
higher price. And no one is willing to sell at a lower-than-market
price when he can sell at a higher one, though there are some who
would be willing to buy at that lower price. So no additional voluntary exchanges are possible. One way to think of freedom is as the
right of the individual to choose his own behavior without constraint
so long as he does not interfere with others. On that definition the
market provides a maximum of freedom; for at the equilibrium point
he must stop. He can go beyond that point only by interfering with
the voluntary choice of others. This suggests that if all markets were
in equilibrium, freedom in the above sense would be maximized
for all participants in the economy, at least over the range of their
economic activity.

To assert that the market economy maximizes freedom of economic
choice is a strong statement. There are important qualifications to
this statement, but it is nonetheless a cogent argument. Lest the reader
be too easily convinced, however, we may mention one qualification.
Not everyone would accept the definition of freedom used in the
preceding paragraph. Many argue that an important freedom is the

freedom from hunger. This, too, is a perfectly legitimate use of the word. But by this definition the market economy may well fail. A man without resources can make no deals; he and his family may starve to death even though all markets are in equilibrium and range-of-choice freedom is maximized. It should also be noted that the discussion of this section applied to model markets. Real markets and real decisions are more complex. We will return to the issue later.

Our very simple description of the market has already yielded some fruit. But one thing it has not done is display much of the tremendous variety of ways in which different markets operate. Let us very briefly indicate six ways in which markets may differ from one another.

The Diversity of Markets

Elasticity

We have already considered the price elasticity of demand curves and some of the reasons for differences. Clearly we may use the same concept in dealing with supply, so that variations in the magnitude of supply elasticity are an important aspect of market diversity. In later chapters we will find that there are other elasticities whose variations are important for understanding market behavior. These elasticities relate changes in the exogenous factors to increases and decreases in supply and demand. They provide a quantitative measure of the important of each exogenous factor on the market.

Knowledge of the Market

If the main suppliers of a product are scattered around a city and buyers, too, are scattered, many participants will not know about many of the potential deals. This tends to reduce the pressures which move the market toward its equilibrium point. In such markets there may be a range of prices over which actual deals are made and which tends to persist over fairly long periods of time. Also there may be not only ignorance but misinformation, as will be discussed in Chapters 4 and 9.

Uncertainty

Uncertainty is closely related to knowledge. A potential buyer is uncertain as to what the going price of a product is. He may be unwilling to put a lot of time or effort into becoming informed and so take the price offered by the first potential seller he meets. His uncertainty stems from his ignorance and so has quite a similar effect. For example, uncertainty is one reason why prices for similar used cars may vary considerably from one used car lot to the next.

Sluggishness of Response

In some markets producers may be afraid of price changes. For example, if there are only a few sellers of a product, any one seller may fear that if he cuts his price he will set off a price war and lose far more than his possible gains from lowering price. He may also figure that if he raises price he will lose his customers to his competitors because they will not follow his lead. Such *oligopoly markets* (few sellers), as they are called, generally have a slower price response to excess supply or demand than in markets where there is more competition.

Stability

This factor has already been considered, and will be taken up again in a broader context in Chapter 10.

External Effects

The consumption of some goods affects the well-being of several people. An extreme example is a collective good such as national defense. When an increase in this service occurs, the amount of defense "consumed" by the entire populace increases. It is not inconceivable that goods of this kind be sold on a market. But it is also true, as we shall see, that markets do not do a good job of providing such goods.

All differences among markets can be subsumed under some combination of these factors. A great deal of economics, in fact, is concerned with understanding the effects of these diverse situations on economic outcomes. The appropriate public policy toward any given market can hardly be determined until the way in which the market operates is understood. Thus whether one is interested in the market as a consumer, a businessman, or as a citizen, the analysis of market behavior is of fundamental importance.

4

Consumption

Households are the most numerous of the economic decision units described in Chapter 2. They are also the most fundamental in the sense that the primary function of the economy is widely regarded to be the providing of households with the appropriate goods and services over the long run. In modern economics about two thirds of the goods and services produced during the course of a year are consumed by households during that year. In this chapter we analyze some aspects of consumer decision making with a view to understanding public policy issues related to consumption.

In Chapter 3 we emphasized the voluntary aspects of exchange in a market economy, and suggested that since each participant in the market has the opportunity to say "No deal," he expects to be made better off when he does make a deal. This in turn suggested that, if no more deals can be made, a kind of optimum has been reached in which no one can find any way to improve his own position without hurting someone else. However, before this suggestion can be given much credence a number of conditions must be satisfied. Most of this book is devoted to discussing these conditions and the means available to achieve them. With respect to consumer decisions we will now be going behind the demand curves

Consumer Satisfaction

of the preceding chapter to see how they may be related to consumer welfare and how consumers respond to various changes in their environment of choice.

Psychologists have not yet succeeded in developing a powerful and generally accepted theory of human motivation. We know that a variety of complex emotions may be involved in the making of a choice between even such simple alternatives as various brands of cigarettes and automobiles, but psychologists are not very adept at assessing the relative importance of these emotions or motivations. Fortunately economists do not need to have very detailed descriptions of motivation for most of their work. The term *satisfaction maximization* is a kind of catchall term for these motivations, one that summarizes a very complex process so as to permit economists to concentrate their attention on matters more directly related to the economic process. But the economist's use of this catchall term not only involves simplification; it also implies certain things about behavior. One of these implicit assumptions is consistency, which for economic choice implies the following. Suppose a consumer has a choice among three bundles of good, A, B, and C. Consistency means that if the consumer preferrs A to B and B to C, then he will also prefer A to C. Thus we imply that our satisfaction motivation permits consumers to rank such alternative bundles of goods, that is, to make a list in which each bundle on the list is preferred to all bundles below it. Occasionally we may also assume that the consumer can rank intensities of satisfaction; for example, he may feel that "moving up" from a Chevrolet to a Cadillac increases his satisfaction by more than moving up to L&M from, say, Camels. But often this assumption can be avoided. Of course different consumers may feel differently. And consistency is assumed to be a property of individual choice, not necessarily of the aggregate choices of a group.

Another important assumption is that there is some stability in these rankings of bundles of goods in terms of satisfaction. If this were not the case much of the analysis of this chapter would be pointless and we would be forced to seek a deeper understanding of the determinants of satisfaction before proceeding. If consumer rankings were constantly and dramatically changing, an analysis of the effects of various situations with respect to any fixed set of rankings for consumers would contribute little to the understanding of consumer behavior.

Some other assumptions are implicit in the use of satisfaction rankings but they can be dealt with later. We will also have to deal later with the issue of the reasonableness of the assumptions we have already made. At the moment let us consider only one possible objection. Impulse buying seems to violate one or the other of the above assumptions. A typical case of impulse buying would be one in which a consumer suddenly chose bundle C above, even though A (and perhaps B as well) was available. This might be interpreted as inconsistency or it might be interpreted as a sudden and perhaps temporary shift in the consumer's satisfaction ranking of bundles. Given that this occurs, our approach may still be useful if impulse buying does not occur too frequently or is common only for relatively minor choices. This means that we will be content with approximate measures of the consequences of different situations.

As a first step we need a way of characterizing the alternatives open to a consumer. We may think in terms of the allocation of a fixed monthly income by a consumer who will be dealing in markets which are in equilibrium and in which he is in each case a minor participant. Thus the consumer must take market prices as given. We will also assume that all goods are divisible into very small (with respect to income) units so that our problem will not be complicated by the lumpiness of some purchases. Finally, we will deal with only two goods in our example. In this case the assumption is purely

The Budget Line

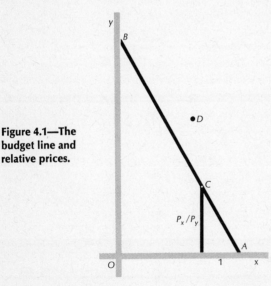

Figure 4.1—The budget line and relative prices.

one of convenience. All our conclusions apply also to the case of a large number of consumer goods.

Figure 4.1 illustrates the alternatives open to a consumer whose money income is I dollars and who will allocate this income over only two goods, x and y, which sell at prices p_x and p_y respectively. Suppose, for example, that his income I is $100 and that $p_x = \$10$ and p_y

$= \$4$. One possibility open to the consumer is to spend all his income on x so that he would have no y and 10 of x. This is bundle A on the diagram. Bundle B represents the maximum possible purchase of y, 25 units.

The most likely alternatives, however, involve purchase of some of each good. Consider an alternative that differs from A in that one less unit of x is bought and this saving is all spent on y. This will give him bundle C which contains p_x/p_y or $2^{1}/_{2}$ units of y and 9 units of x. Notice that if he spends all his income, adjustments in the relative amounts of each good are always in the same proportions (p_x/p_y) regardless of the amounts in the initial bundles. This means that the line showing all these possible bundles has constant slope, or steepness, for p_x/p_y measures marginal or small changes in the composition of the bundles and consequently the steepness of the line. A line with constant slope is a straight line, as drawn in Figure 4.1.

Clearly the consumer could not have more of both x and y than is contained in any bundle on the line AB, for then he would be spending more than his monthly income. For this reason AB is called the *budget line*, since it shows the maximum amounts of x and y the consumer can obtain with his income. The algebraic version of AB is: $p_x x + p_y y = I$. Notice that in our diagrammatic version the values of x and y appear explicitly, the prices appear only as a ratio determining the slope of the line, and I does not appear explicitly. I does serve to fix the distance of AB from the origin, however. If income were larger the consumer could purchase more of both x and y, say D, and so the line would lie farther out.[1]

Actually our consumer could choose any bundle lying inside or on the edges of the triangle AOB. For example, he could choose point O, buying none of either x or y and saving his money. But saving is a kind of consumer good too, since it gives the consumer the opportunity to buy more goods in the future. Thus in order really to restrict our example to the case of two goods we assume that all income is spent on one or both of the goods. This means that our consumer's range of choice covers every bundle of goods which lies on AB, and no others.

▶ *The budget line is the set of all bundles of goods that may be purchased at fixed prices with a given sum of money.*

▶▶ *The budget line is a straight line—that is, the same small change may be made in the composition of a bundle of goods regardless of the composition of that bundle before the change.*

1. Notice that if income were just sufficient to permit purchase of bundle D, the new budget line would be parallel to AB. This is because prices have not changed and so their ratio, p_x/p_y, determines the slope of both budget lines.

► ► *The slope of the budget line is determined by the price ratio of the goods.*

The consumer will choose that point on AB which gives him the most satisfaction. Given his satisfaction ranking, we can say something about the nature of this point. It has the property that an additional dollar spent on either good must give the same additional satisfaction. If this were not the case the consumer could increase his satisfaction by spending a dollar less on the good that gave less additional satisfaction and a dollar more on the other. There is, however, one important proviso to this rule: it applies only to goods that are actually consumed. At point A the consumer might still get less satisfaction from a dollar's worth of y than from a dollar's worth of x, but unfortunately he can do no more substituting.

► ► *The bundle of goods that gives the consumer most satisfaction has the property that, for all goods actually consumed, the additional satisfaction gained from an additional dollar expenditure on each good is the same.*

The above is another of those marginal-adjustment rules which play such an important role in economic analysis. Another one—the rule of optimal exchange—was given in Chapter 3. The similarities between these two rules are striking. In both cases they do not tell you how to get to the optimum, but only what it is like once you are there. The optimal-exchange rule only told you what it was like if no more deals could be consummated; the latest rule tells you what it is like if household income has been spent to best advantage. Both rules deal with small-scale movements from the optimum in a number of directions—the first with exchanges of good between households, the second with shifts in spending from one good to another. This suggests that there may be other possibilities for improvement that have not been taken into account. These would be situations in which one misses the forest for the trees, missing opportunities for improvement by means of large-scale adjustment because these opportunities are quite different from those near the defined optimum. Only a comparison of all possible bundles of goods can be sufficient to guarantee that such an outcome does not exist.

The analytic framework that has just been developed can now be used to illustrate the response of a consumer to changes in his environment of choice. First consider changes in money income with prices of the consumer goods remaining unchanged. This means a parallel shift in line AB of Figure 4.1. The shift is parallel because p_x and p_y, which fix the slope of the budget line for each level of money income, have not changed. For each such line the consumer will

Spending Responses to Changes in Income

choose a particular bill of consumption, namely, the bundle that satisfies our optimal-adjustment rule. These points have been traced out in Figure 4.2 and connected by the line CC'C".

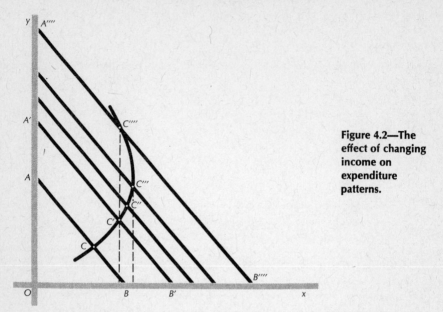

Figure 4.2—The effect of changing income on expenditure patterns.

By and large we would expect that an increase in income will lead to an increase in the consumption of most goods, but we would not expect the increase to occur in the same proportions for each good. Thus as incomes rise we would expect expenditures on both food and clothing to rise, but, at least beyond some point, food expenditures would probably rise more slowly than clothing expenditures and expenditures on leisure time activities. Income consumption lines like CC'C" can be used to measure these changes. However, economists do not attempt to measure such changes for individual households. Instead they have tried to develop aggregative measures of the changes. All households may be grouped into income classes and the budget allocations of households in each income class averaged to get a measure of the typical pattern of consumption for each income group. Differences in budget allocations between income classes can then be found. Figure 4.3 shows some actual measures of these aggregate income-consumption lines, generally called Engel curves after their inventor. Because they are aggregative measures and are based on cross sections of households having different incomes in a particular year, they are not precise measures of how particular consumers will behave as their income increases. For example, a large proportion of the lower-income group mem-

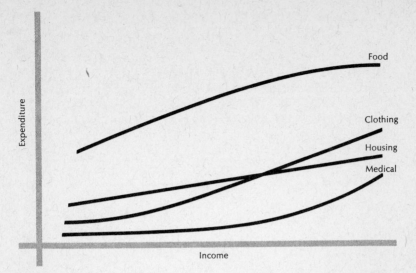

Figure 4.3—Engel curves, showing how expenditure patterns vary with income.

bers have lower levels of education than higher-income group members. When some of the former enjoy an increase in their incomes they may not increase their expenditures on some goods, such as books, by as much as the aggregate Engel curve would suggest. However, Engel curves are a useful approximate measure of consumer response to income changes. And of course by finer breakdowns of consumers into groups the effects of such things as family size and education can be taken into account.

In order to compare the degree of responsiveness of consumer expenditures to income changes a measure has been developed which is a partner to the price elasticity concept studied in Chapter 3.

▶ *The income elasticity of demand for a good is the ratio of the percentage change in consumer expenditure on that good to a given small percentage change in money income, with prices remaining constant.*

As with the price elasticities of demand, the income elasticity is independent of the units chosen to measure amounts of the good,[2] so that comparisons among goods and among consumer groups are meaningful. A high income elasticity for a good means a relatively large response in spending on that good when income changes.

Table 4.1 shows some empirical estimates of price and income elas-

2. The measure is also independent of the money unit chosen. Not only can either dollars or cents be used, but also dollars or francs, thus permitting international comparisons of consumer behavior using this concept. Nevertheless there are many serious problems of interpretation with international comparisons. For example, it is difficult to isolate comparable income classes between two countries. Also price ratios may be different and income elasticities can obviously be different for the same consumer and the same goods if the price ratios change.

ticities. Notice that all the price elasticities are negative, indicating that an increase in price leads to a decrease in consumption, and vice versa.[3] This is not surprising. However, not all the income elas-

Table 4.1—Some Empirical Price and Income Elasticities of Demand

Good	Income elasticity	Price elasticity
Food	0.3	—0.3
Cream	1.7	—1.3
Beer	—0.1	—0.9
Clothing	1.0	—0.5
Rent	1.8	—1.4

ticities are positive. A negative income elasticity means that an increase in income leads to a decrease in the consumption of that good, and vice versa. Though most goods have positive income elasticities, there is a fairly important class of goods for which this is not true.

► *Inferior goods have, over some range of incomes, a negative income elasticity.*

Margarine is the classic case of an inferior good. Many people prefer butter but at low incomes feel they cannot afford it. However, a rise in income makes butter consumption more feasible and so the amount of margarine that is bought may actually be reduced. A more important case is bread consumption at low incomes. Suppose bread is the staple food of a poor family which can afford a certain amount of meat, a much more expensive food, as a supplement to the family diet. If income now falls the family, in order to survive, must cut back meat consumption and increase the purchase of bread. If income rises, the reverse process may occur and bread consumption decline. It should be noted that negative income elasticities can occur only over a limited range of incomes. Logical limits are set by the fact that no more than *I* can be spent on the good and no less than none of it can be bought. In Figure 4.3 good *x* is inferior over the two highest income levels shown on the diagram, but good *y* is not inferior.

Spending Responses to Changes in Price The connection between individual consumer budget allocations and product demand curves can be made a bit more explicitly by means of budget line analysis. Figure 4.4 shows a consumer's reaction to changes in p_x, with p_y and money income *I*, remaining con-

3. Because this is almost always true of price elasticities of demand, economists often do not bother to write down the sign. But see below, pp. 43-44. The data in Table 4.1 are international averages, which accounts for the different values for food here and at p. 27.

Figure 4.4—The effect of changing price on expenditure patterns.

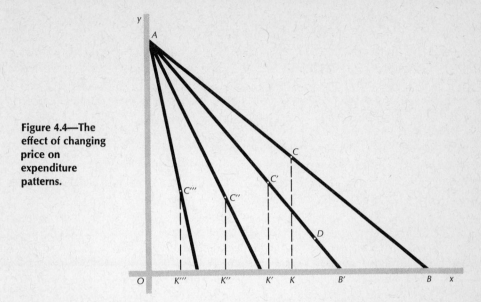

stant. To see how the diagram works, note that when the budget line becomes steeper the slope is greater so that p_x/p_y has increased. Since the same amount of y can be bought on on AB' as on AB when none of x is bought, neither income nor the price of y have changed.[4] Thus a rotation of AB about point A such as occurs on the diagram shows successive increases in p_x with p_y and I remaining constant.

The points C, C', C'', which show maximum-satisfaction bundles of goods, together with the budget line, provide the information necessary to construct the individual consumer's demand curve. For the given p_y the slope of AB determines p_x and the horizontal distance OK determines the amount the consumer will purchase. When p_x is raised to the value indicated by the slope of AB' the amount demanded is reduced to OK', and so forth. If we had this information for all consumers we could add the amounts of x demanded by each consumer at any given price and we would have a point on a demand curve. Note that, in agreement with Chapter 3, such a demand curve would be constructed on the assumption that money income and the prices of other goods were held constant.

No one has yet attempted to construct a demand curve for a product in this way. The amount of information that would be required to generate even a single demand curve by this process would be quite overwhelming. However, it is useful to see that there is a connection between these two aspects of consumption analysis. Also

4. We ignore the redundant possibility of matching changes in I and p_y, which in this case would produce the same kind of change in the budget line

it is possible to suggest an unexpected aspect of demand analysis. Notice that we might conceivably have found in Figure 4.4 that the initial increase in p_x led the consumer to shift his consumption bundle from C to D. If this had happened it would have meant that an increase in price led to an *increase* in consumption. Is this ever possible? The logical answer is that it may happen, but, just as we have drawn it, only in cases where there is a substantial negative income elasticity. If the price of good x rises this creates a tendency to substitute other goods for it. If there is a positive income elasticity the tendency to consume less of x is reinforced. This is because real income decreases when price rises, real income being interpreted as the command of a consumer over goods and services rather than simply the amount of money he has. When the price rises the consumer can no longer buy the bundle of goods he preferred before the rise. So the positive income elasticity leads him also to consume less of the good. However, if income elasticity is negative the effect of the real-income change works against the "substitution effect" of the price change. If it is strong enough to overcome the latter, the amount demanded may actually rise with a rise in price.

► ► *Demand curves always slope downward for goods with positive income elasticities. Only if there is a strong negative income elasticity can a demand curve be upward sloping.*

In practice, product-demand curves that are upward sloping over part of their length are extremely rare. A principal reason for this is that a product-demand curve aggregates the individual demand curves of consumers having a very wide range of incomes. Since income elasticities are negative only over a limited range of incomes the limited number of individuals who have strong enough negative income elasticities for the good tend to be swamped by the mass of consumers with weakly negative and positive income elasticities.

Income and Satisfaction
Two kinds of income were defined in the last section. Money income is the amount of money received by a decision unit over some given time period. Its usefulness in analyzing household behavior has already been illustrated. Real income was also defined: it measures the ability a decision unit acquires over some given time period to obtain goods and services. The real-income concept is more fundamental than that of money income, since it takes account of the effects on the household budget of general price changes. If money income doubles at the same time that all prices double, real income has not changed. However, when prices are stable, money income can serve as a good measure of real income. In what follows we will use the single word "income" to stand for real income.

Income measures the ability of a household to acquire goods while satisfaction measures the impact of goods acquired on the household. The one concept refers to the range of alternatives open to a household, the other to the consequences of making a particular choice. Since we expect households to exercise their command over goods there should be a close relation between income and satisfaction. However, the two concepts are far from being identical. Let us first consider the relationship with respect to a household treated, as usual, as a single, integrated decision unit.

Three propositions have often been put forward as being generally consistent with our experience of individual satisfaction:

1. With respect to real income, individuals quite generally prefer more to less regardless of their present level of consumption. In effect, man is insatiable: no one has so much that he could not have his satisfaction increased by some conceivable increase in consumption.

2. With respect to any particular consumer good, man is satiable. In particular, the additional satisfaction gained as a result of the consumption of an additional unit of the good tends to decrease with increases in the amount available for consumption. This is often called the *principle of diminishing marginal utility,* since yet another application of the marginal principle is involved.[5]

3. As income increases, the satisfaction generated by an additional dollar of income tends to decline. This is often called the *principle of diminishing marginal utility of income.*

The first of these propositions suggests a reason why goods generally continue to be valuable even though their supply has greatly increased. If pushed to its limit it also suggests that a society of general abundance, in which everyone will have all the goods and services he wants, will never occur. For this reason it has sometimes been attacked. A more common line of attack on it says that people do not need more than a modest level of affluence and should be encouraged, trained, perhaps even indoctrinated to be satisfied with this modest affluence. The implication of this is that the argument that markets provide a maximum of welfare consistent with freedom is false. It is false because the modestly affluent participants are wrong in thinking they are better off when increasing their consumption as a result of making deals on the markets. If this is accepted, our market analysis may still provide a good description of behavior, but it can no longer be said to have any normative content.

The second proposition is less frequently attacked as being false. Some would emphasize that there may be a significant range over

5. The word "utility" is most commonly employed to designate satisfaction. We are using the somewhat more neutral word "satisfaction" in this chapter in an effort to emphasize the very complex and at the same time diffuse nature of the concept.

which additional units provide increasing satisfaction. An example might be additional pairs of shoes after the first. Given that one can go shod, one's interest in being fashionable may be such that the diversity of wear possible when one moves from two to three pairs of shoes provides a marginal additional satisfaction greater than the increase that occurred when a second pair was added to the wardrobe.[6] A more fundamental criticism of the proposition is that it implies too much about satisfaction. Satisfaction, it is asserted, is rather like temperature: 64° Fahrenheit is not twice as high a temperature as 32° in any meaningful sense, as is suggested by the fact that in many countries the centigrade scale is used, in which the temperature corresponding to 64° is infinitely many times higher than that corresponding to 32° (which is 0°C.). Similarly with satisfaction, it is not possible to make comparable assertions about the amount of satisfaction produced by a change in the composition of a bundle of goods. We cannot go into this question in detail. The important thing to note is that nearly everything economic analysts have wished to say about satisfaction can be said without making statements like "This satisfaction level is twice that," but that it is often easier to speak as if such statements were acceptable. We will follow the latter course, even though running the risk of proving too much with the additional assumption.

Our third proposition probably seems plausible enough. Who would deny that an additional dollar granted to a family provides more satisfaction if the family is starving than if it is very rich?

However, there is a consideration which casts some doubt on the third proposition. Suppose that the satisfactions of consumers are not mutually independent. My satisfaction depends not only on the goods I consume but also to some extent on those that you consume. Charity and keeping up with the Joneses are possible instances of this situation. One aspect of keeping up with the Joneses is that my satisfaction is now tied to Jones' and perhaps to that of the other families in my neighborhood or social circle. If my income is much less than Jones', then I may be desperately eager to increase it so as to consume similar goods to those my friends consume and thereby help establish my solidarity with them. But before I moved to the Jones' neighborhood I lived in an area where consumption was at a lower level than mine. I still enjoyed increases in income but not nearly so much as I would now. In this case my marginal utility of income may actually increase until I can get closer to Jones' spending style.

One additional point may be made about interdependence in con-

6. As always we are comparing equilibrium positions. The best possible two-pair combination is being compared, *ceteris paribus*, with the best possible three-pair combination. The principle's defenders might reply that different kinds of shoes are different goods, so the objection is irrelevant.

sumption. One may describe this situation by saying that the relevant consumer goods, such as cars, furnishings, and clothes, create external effects. Jones' new car may have affected my satisfaction adversely, since it tends to put me still farther behind in the race. It is rather like smog in its effect on me. I did not participate in the deal that reduced my satisfaction. As will be discussed later on, goods of this kind pose particularly difficult problems for economic analysis.

Thus we see that the relation between income and satisfaction is quite complex. It is not even always true that they both tend to move in the same direction. Note, too, that we have been dealing with the relation with respect to a single household. Economists often use measures of the total income of a group of households. Such measures are very crude, since a set of "abilities to command goods and services" are rather hard things to add together. The problem with total satisfaction is even greater, however, since we have nothing like money income (corrected for price changes) to use as a readily available if crude approximation.

In concluding this section let us consider briefly a well-known proposal relating to income distribution in a society. The proposal is that social policy be oriented toward producing the maximum total satisfaction over all households in the economy. If we cannot measure satisfaction, what is the implication of applying this criterion? Suppose we make two additional assumptions: (1) human nature makes human beings sufficiently alike that it can be safely assumed that people are essentially equal in their capacity to derive satisfaction from given situations; and (2) the marginal utility of income is declining. This would seem to suggest that equality of income will produce the most utility. For any readjustment of income which took from the rich, with their low marginal utility of income, and gave to the high-marginal-utility-of-income poor would increase total satisfaction. The transfer of a dollar takes less satisfaction from the rich than it confers on the poor.

This argument illustrates the importance of equilibrium analysis. It shows how, using this analysis, a striking conclusion about how to maximize satisfaction can be reached even though we have no specific measure of satisfaction. Of course objections may be raised against both the proposed criterion and the two additional assumptions, some of which we have already considered. Unfortunately there is another assumption buried in the argument which is probably more damaging to it than any of these objections. This is the assumption that the transfer of income does not affect the total amount of goods and services available. Suppose that, if everyone had the same income, incentives to work would be reduced so that, on the average, individuals were only half as productive as before equality was established. A large majority of people would have much less income than before the change and perhaps not so many would have more. Whether or not the equality-is-best rule can survive these objections depends partly on one's own values and partly on the factual question of the effect of equality on motivation. We return to this question of income distribution in later chapters.

Risk and
Satisfaction

Up to now we have been assuming that the consumer knows exactly what the consequences of a decision will be. But in practice this is rarely the case. If he is considering buying a house, he does not know for certain whether it will burn down, be appropriated by the state to build a freeway, double in value as the result of a local real estate boom, or remain indefinitely in pretty much the same economic condition in which he buys it. Similar risks lie behind nearly all prospective purchases of consumer goods and employment choices. How does a consumer make decisions so as to get the most satisfaction from his budget allocations when risk enters into his decisions?

► *We will call a risky alternative, one in which the consequences of choosing it are uncertain, a bet.*

Consider first a simple case in which the risks are known. The decision involves two alternatives. The first is to do nothing and retain one's present income with certainty. The second is to accept a single bet which gives one an even chance of winning or losing $100, depending on the flip of a coin. The decision then is whether or not to make the bet.

In our fifty-fifty bet the probability of winning and of losing is .5 in each case. Now an important factor in making a decision involving risk is the likelihood of winning and losing if the same bet is chosen a large number of times. The amount of average winnings or losses when this is done gives a useful piece of information as to whether or not to make the bet. In our bet we have two possible outcomes, winning and losing, which are mutually exclusive, since you cannot both win and lose at the same time. The two events are also exhaustive, that is, given that you choose to bet, winning and losing are the only possible outcomes. The average winnings in a large number of bets is now determined by the expected value of the bet.

► *The expected value of a set of exhaustive, mutually exclusive outcomes is the sum of the products of the probability of each event times its payoff:*

$$E = \sum_{i=1} P_i l_i,$$

where I_i is the amount won or lost if outcome i occurs and P_i is the probability that outcome i will occur.

So the value of each outcome to the bettor is weighted by the likelihood that it will occur. Note also that the sum of the probabilities is 1, since exactly one of these alternatives must occur.

In our example we have: $E = (.5) \times (100) + (.5) \times (-100) = 50 - 50 = 0$. On the average you will neither win nor lose if you make a large number of these bets, a not unexpected outcome. Using the concept of expected value we can now construct a rather formalistic definition of a gamble.

► *A gamble is the choice of the second alternative in the following situation. Two alternatives are available: to keep a given income with certainty, ceteris paribus, or to accept a bet whose expected value is no greater than that income.*

The second alternative in our example is a gamble. If the loss were $110 instead of 100 we would have: $E = (.5) \times (100) + (.5) \times (110) = 50 - 55 = -5$. This is still a gamble. But if the payoffs were reversed, E would be $+5$ and it would no longer be a gamble. Notice that, ignoring skill, most games of chance are gambles. This is especially true of games at professional gambling houses where the house takes a percentage from each game so that the expected value of each game is negative. So too is the expected value of gambling at a professional house, regardless of the game. Notice also that, according to our definition, professional gamblers do not gamble, because they can be expected to win.

Now let us return to the case of an individual whose marginal utility of income decreases with increasing income. To take account of risk we can rephrase his situation to say that it is the marginal utility of the expected value of his income which is decreasing. This is a somewhat more general statement than the earlier one, since it includes the earlier statement as a special case. If only certain (i.e., sure) alternatives are being considered, $E = 1 \times I$ for each alternative, and the rule works out as before. But in our extended case we have the following conclusion.

►► *An individual whose marginal utility of expected income is decreasing will never choose a gamble.*

The reasoning follows the same line as in the certain income case. In our initial case of $100 won or lost, because of decreasing marginal utility of income, the satisfaction gained from winning $100 is less than the satisfaction foregone by losing $100. Therefore, though the bet is "fair" in terms of dollars, it is unfair in terms of satisfaction.

49

Let us consider now a case of fire insurance. A house is worth $10,000. It may be fully insured against fire risk for $100. The consumer figures that the risk of burning with complete loss over the period of the policy is one in a hundred or .01 and that all other risks have zero probability. Should he insure, given that his marginal utility of income is decreasing?

Our consumer faces two alternatives:

Alternative 1

Insure: Yields a certain income of $10,000 − 200 = $9,800

Alternative 2

Not insure: Either save $200 premium with probability .99
or lose house ($10,000) with probability .01.

In alternative 2, the expected value of the "bet," which is the same as his expected income, is:

$$E = (.99) \times (10,000) + (.01) \times (-10,000) = 9,900 - 100 = \$9,800$$

Thus *not* taking out insurance is a gamble and he will insure. Clearly for any premium that does not exceed $200 the consumer will insure. He may insure even if the premium is above $200, though insuring would no longer be a gamble, provided his marginal utility of income is decreasing rapidly enough.

So far so good. But now we must face the fact that many consumers not only take out insurance but also take gambles. This can be partly explained as the pleasure of playing the game. Poker is a social activity as well as a set of gambles, though for the good player the game may not be too much of a gamble. To some extent this "play" aspect of satisfaction carries over into economic activities, as in the case of many players in the stock market.[7] But for most economic activities playing the game is not particularly pleasurable in itself, so some other explanation is needed.

This takes us to our new version of the argument of the preceding section, which said that there may be ranges of incomes over which the marginal utility of expected income is increasing with income. In this case the net satisfaction gained from a fair or zero-expected-value bet is *greater* than that of the certain-income alternative. The consumer engaged in keeping up with the Joneses will buy fire insurance for his house because for much lower incomes his marginal utility of expected income is decreasing. But he may also buy lottery tickets regularly because over some higher incomes it is increasing. Eventually the marginal utility must start to decrease again or he

7. The proposition about gambling could still hold, but the consumer would have to add to the expected income of the bet an amount to compensate the satisfaction of playing.

would only gamble for the longest odds with the money he allocates to risky attempts to increase his income.

Making gambles involving a limited portion of income in an effort to increase income substantially may be reflected in a variety of economic decisions. One example might be choosing a career in which only a few are very successful while the remainder tend to have incomes lower than the average of alternative careers. A career as an advertising executive compared to that of a dentist may be a case in point. The assigning of a portion of one's investment portfolio for speculative ventures is another.

The insurance example shows that the economic role of insurance is to make it possible for consumers to avoid gambles. In practice, however, it is not usually possible for the consumer to shift all the risk. Partly there is an incentive problem. Unless the consumer shares some of the risks of his house burning he has no incentive to take precautionary measures. But there is also the problem that the nature of many risks is highly uncertain. Often the probabilities of the various outcomes are not known, so that the expected value of the alternative cannot be calculated with any confidence. The consumer can hardly shift the risk if he does not know what it is. This is part of the problem of economic information, to which we now turn.

Consumers in a modern society face a tremendous number of alternatives and have a very large number of decisions to make with respect to these alternative uses of time and money. Full consideration of the alternatives means that a fair amount of knowledge is needed for each decision. At the same time the human brain is limited in its capacity to store, recall, and process information, and human will power and patience in performing these tasks is limited. How does all this affect choice?

Knowledge and Satisfaction

In such a situation the individual must find ways to save on the information costs of decision making. Several familiar aspects of human behavior are closely associated with information saving. The first and simplest is habit. One gets into the habit of reading the newspaper at the breakfast table or of putting one's pants on before one's shirt, which means that a pair of deliberative decisions is avoided each morning. Similarly with budget allocations, one gets into the habit of grocery shopping twice a week or of purchasing a particular brand and amount of tobacco without giving careful consideration to questions of one's present stocks and prospective needs. Habit often extends to a choice of shops in which to make purchases, thereby eliminating the time-consuming process of making price comparisons over a range of potential deals.

A second aspect of human behavior associated with information saving is the use of rules of thumb. Instead of solving a problem completely, one applies a rule of choice which is used whenever this particular class of decisions comes up. A housewife may buy only the most expensive brands of canned goods, which involves the application of a rule of thumb, and may then use some of the time saved to haggle with the butcher over cuts and prices of meat.

A third important information saver is the closed mind. Many alternatives which are relevant for a decision are simply excluded from consideration. One behaves as if certain stores or lines of goods or methods of purchase do not exist, even though in fact they do, and by so doing one avoids the necessity of comparing these alternatives with others.

All three of these types of behavior may be wholly conscious and deliberately constructed. But it seems likely that this is not frequently the case. Instead the behavior has been absorbed intuitively from one's own experience and the experience of others. We are often not fully aware of the implications of our behavior. In addition we may not follow the procedures with perfect consistency, being occasionally sidetracked by some new experience or impulse. This raises the question as to whether the consumer can reasonably be thought to behave in a rational and consistent way, as we have been assuming up to now.

We cannot hope to give a satisfactory empirical answer to this question here. Perhaps it will help to pose the issue within the framework of consumer analysis which we have been using to this point. To do so we interpose a new concept between the consumer good and the consumer's satisfaction. This is the notion of the characteristics of a good which make it attractive to the consumer. Thus it is

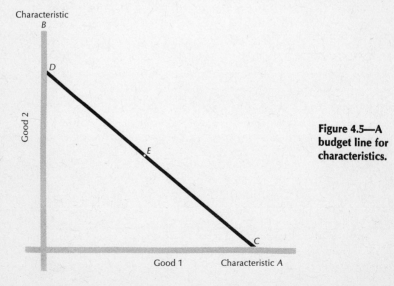

Figure 4.5—A budget line for characteristics.

not the consumer good itself which gives satisfaction but its charac-teristics. For example, the color and juiciness and "worminess" of an apple are three characteristics of that fruit which give satisfaction—and of course dissatisfaction. Some goods such as automobiles may possess a very large number of characteristics which are relevant for a given consumer. Others, such as writing paper, may have only two or three.

In Figure 4.5 a special case is depicted. There are two character-istics, A and B, and they are independent of one another so that the amount of satisfaction generated by one is not dependent on the amount of the other that is present. In addition the amount of the characteristic present is assumed to be proportional to the amount of the good the consumer possesses. Let us assume first that there are two goods, 1 and 2, which each possess only one characteristic, A in the case of good 1, and B in the case of good 2. Now consider allocating a fixed money income between the two goods. Given prices, if the individual spends all his money on good 1 he acquires OC of characteristic A and none of B, and if he spends it all on good 2 he gets OD of characteristic B and none of A. Because of our pro-portionality assumption, he has a straight budget line, CD, with re-spect to the characteristics, which shows the possible combinations of A and B he can achieve with his income. Suppose that maximum satisfaction is achieved at point E on CD.

Now let us turn to Figure 4.6 and assume that there is another good, number 3, which possesses both characteristics in some fixed propor-

Figure 4.6—The characteristics budget line can be bent.

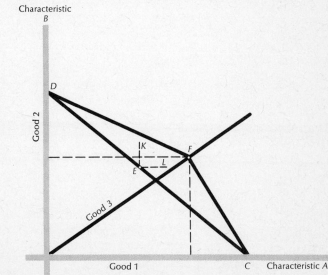

53

tion. This good has a low enough price (or a large enough supply of the characteristics per unit of the good) that the consumer can get out to point *F* if he spends all his money on good 3. Clearly he would be better off to do so, since he would then get more of each characteristic than if he bought the combination of goods 1 and 2 represented by *E*.[8] Notice that if the consumer knows about this good then it follows that he will never buy both goods 1 and 2. For if his satisfaction leans more toward *B* than *A* he can always do better with a combination of goods 2 and 3 than with 1 and 2; the same advantage applies to 1 and 3 over 1 and 2 if his tastes lie relatively more in the direction of *A*. With good 3 in the picture, our consumer's budget line for characteristics has become bent in the middle. It is now *CFD*.

Someone who uses habit or rules of thumb or closed-mindedness in budget decisions certainly runs the risk of missing goods like number 3. In addition, advertising practices may encourage him in this direction. Confusing weight and volume reporting, misleading packaging and the use of pseudoscientific jargon in describing products may increase information costs to the consumer to the point where he will not believe it worthwhile to try good 3; or the advertising may convince him without trial that its characteristics for him are different than they in fact are.

► ►   *The multiplying of goods differing only slightly in their characteristics may not increase consumers' welfare by expanding their range of choice but reduce welfare as a consequence of less efficient consumer decision making.*

Having pointed to a variety of ways in which consumer behavior may be inefficient and irrational, it seems desirable to close on a more positive note, since models based on the assumption of reasonably consistent consumer behavior play an important role in economics. All the information saving devices we have mentioned can be "rationalized," that is, they can be interpreted as making the consumer a better decision maker than he would otherwise be. Central to this argument is the concept of adjustment at the margin. Neither in retail markets nor in others is everyone constantly down in the market place bargaining for a better deal and eagerly policing deviations from the equilibrium price. Instead, adjustments in markets take place at the margin. A few of the participants become dissatisfied with the status quo and seek to bring about change; they test the market, so to speak. If the market is indeed ripe for change their test is a success and price is adjusted. If not the test fails and the old

8. All points to the right of *KE* and above *LE* yield more of both characteristics than does *E*.

price continues. But most participants in most markets are passive price takers most of the time.

So it is with consumer budget allocation. The existing state of affairs is a rough-and-ready distillation of knowledge and experience accumulated over the years. Because of this there is a presumption of success about it, a presumption that the innumerable tests in the past have adjusted behavior in the direction of optimal satisfaction, even though it has not yet been reached. But occasionally some consumers come to question the satisfaction generated by current behavior. They test the market, trying a new brand or perhaps a radically different product which may have relatively more of the desired characteristics (one sells the golf clubs and buys a sailboat). If the test is a success, a new behavior pattern emerges which improves on the old, and information about the change may percolate to other decision units, thereby bringing about a perhaps substantial change in consumer behavior.

Nor does advertising always hinder the effort of consumers to achieve satisfaction. A producer whose product's characteristics really will produce satisfaction more efficiently than others may use the media simply to convey this information persuasively. And much advertising conveys useful information about the properties of goods, thus reducing the information cost to consumers. We will return later to this question of whether the market system does a satisfactory job in producing consumer satisfaction.

5

Production

Production is essentially the transformation over time of one set of goods into another. A businessman has a factory and some raw materials and labor and makes additions to these stocks over time. He uses these in his production activities so as to get certain amounts of various kinds of goods. In addition to these goods, at any point in time he still has his factory (slightly more worn perhaps), his employees, and inventories of various raw materials, goods in process of transformation, and products.

Most of these items can be bought and sold on markets.[1] However, there is an aspect of production which is not directly related to markets. This is the technological aspect, the fact that nature and human knowledge set many limits to the kinds of transformations of goods that are possible. The study of these possible transformations and their properties forms much of the subject matter of engineering rather than economics. Yet the economist's interest in economic decisions forces him to acquire some general understanding of the nature of typical transformations of goods, both existing and potential. Obviously the technological alternatives available in an economy

1. One cannot buy a laborer in most countries but one can contract to buy the services of a laborer for some limited period of time.

have an important bearing on the choices of economic decision units. In this chapter we will be looking for simplified ways of describing technology which provide the most relevant technological information for the understanding of economic decision making.

Probably the most difficult analytic problems in economics are those that require a sophisticated treatment of time if they are to be useful. This is certainly true when dealing with the description of production processes. Fortunately, however, it has turned out that many important economic problems can be dealt with effectively by using a highly simplified picture of the role of time in the production process. One of the most common of these is applied in the next section, which deals with the various possible combinations of outputs that can be produced in a given time period. In this case time is divided into only two periods—the current period, which may last for a year, for example, and the future. What happens over time within one of these periods is ignored, or rather it is assumed that everything happens at once within the period. This is a useful simplification when attention is focused on the current period taken as a whole. We will come across other ways of dealing with time later on.

Note that transformations may take place with respect to space and time as well as quality. Shipping a good is a "pure" case of spatial transformation, storing of temporal.

> ▶ *By the production system we mean all the possible transformations of goods that might be chosen by some set of decision makers in a given period of time.*

One such production system is the collection of all possible transformations of goods and services that might be carried out in the American economy next year. Another production system is that of an enterprise for last year; yet another is that of an industry in the second quarter of this year. The idea of transformation leads naturally to a twofold classification of the goods and services that appear in a set of transformations into inputs and outputs. And this in turn leads to a classification of transformations into efficient and inefficient.

> ▶ *Efficient transformations are those in which ceteris paribus: (1) it is not possible to increase the amount of any output without increasing the amount of some input or decreasing the amount of some other output; and (2) it is not possible to decrease the amount of any input without reducing the amount of some output or increasing the amount of some other input. All others are inefficient.*

Efficiency obviously is defined with some given state of technology in mind. Notice, too, that the definition does not explicitly imply any value judgment. One need not be efficient. But of course most of the situations we will be dealing with are ones in which efficiency will be desirable, and in many cases there will be pressures in the environment encouraging the choice of efficient transformations. However, implicitly some normative or value content attaches to the definition. This enters when the choice is made as to what is an input and what is an output. Efficient choices tend, other things equal, to yield more of outputs and to use less of inputs. If labor, for example, were positively valued so that people liked to work and wanted to work more hours than they do, then it might be appropriate to class it as an output. Ordinarily, of course, it is treated as an input. The definition of inputs and outputs determines the particular kind of efficiency measure you will get, and consequently definitions of efficiency are related indirectly to value considerations, to the purposes of the analysis.

Another very useful classification of goods and services is three-fold: factors of production, intermediate goods, and final goods. Later in this chapter a model production system will be described which contains all three of these types of goods. In this system emphasis is placed on what transformations occur within a given time period, so the current-future time period classification is again employed.

► *Final goods are those that flow out of the production system during the period of production.*

For example, in a national economy those goods that are turned over to consumers have flowed out, as have those that are shipped abroad. This is fair enough since neither consumers nor foreigners, as a rule, make domestic production decisions. A third kind of final goods has a less obvious property in common with the other kinds. These are goods that will be useful in the future but are not used up or formally transferred out of the hands of production decision makers during the period. These investment goods, as they are called, consist of factories that are under construction and stocks of goods that are finished but have not yet been transferred out of the system, or are still in the process of transformation. The performance of an economy during a time period is often judged in terms of the total amount of final goods that are produced during the period, the term gross national product being one such concept. Investment goods are included in this category because they are not used for productive purposes during the given time period but will eventually be useful.

► Intermediate goods are those that will be transferred out of the production system but must undergo further transformation before flowing out as part of final demand.

Yarn which has been produced from cotton but will be converted into cloth is an example, as are many products of the steel industry, the components of complex goods like automobiles, and so forth. Many goods may be either final or intermediate. For example, some yarn is transformed into cloth within the production system while other yarn is transferred directly to consumers or goes into producers' stocks. Another example is an automobile, which is often used not as a consumption good but as part of the production system when driven by a salesman or company executive on business.[2]

► Factors of production consist of four special types of inputs into the production process: land, labor, capital, and entrepreneurship.

This is a conventional definition of the basic inputs into the economic system; that is it is not so clear-cut a concept as the other two, but has a long history in economic thought and plays a sufficiently important role in current economic discussions that its role requires some discussion. Most of our discussion of factors of production occurs in Chapter 8, but one point is in order here. It sometimes requires some care to distinguish factors of productions from final products. This is especially true of capital—that is, of reproducible wealth like factories and machinery. In dealing with final goods we treated factories under construction and not yet "on stream" as final goods. Such a factory is not yet a factor of production; it cannot be used this period to transform goods. Hence it is a part of final demand. It is transferred to factor-of-production status when it does come on stream. A similar distinction may be made, for example, between labor at work and labor in training.

Using these concepts we now proceed to describe some important aspects of production systems in modern economies. In the next section is a model which shows the possible combinations of final goods which can be transformed out of some given set of inputs in a particular time period. Then we turn to the relation between inputs and outputs. This is first discussed by means of a simple model which separates economic from technological-production aspects of eco-

2. A wife darning socks might seem to be properly part of the production system. Statisticians do not agree, mainly because the amount of such work is very difficult to measure. Housewives do not report on their efforts to any public agency, and would often have difficulty in distinguishing between housework and leisure. As with many of these classifications, it is very difficult to decide exactly where to draw the line between two "boxes," though the general idea of the classification is reasonable enough.

nomic flows of final goods and factors of production. Then we proceed to a model in which final goods, intermediate goods, and factors of production all make their appearance. Lastly we take another kind of look at the role of prices in simplifying economic decisions.

Transformation and Opportunity Cost

Let us assume that in our production system the amount of inputs available is fixed and that just two different goods can be produced, which we may call F (for factories) and G (for consumer goods). We also assume that factories can be produced during the given time period but that the new factories cannot be used in producing more consumer goods or factories until next period. We are interested in the different combinations of these two goods that the economy is capable of producing. For example, if consumers are future-oriented, that is, are willing to defer present consumption in order to have more goods in the future, and if businessmen know of new and better ways to produce goods, the economy may produce relatively a lot of factories and not so many consumer goods. In an economy oriented more toward present consumption the reverse will be true.

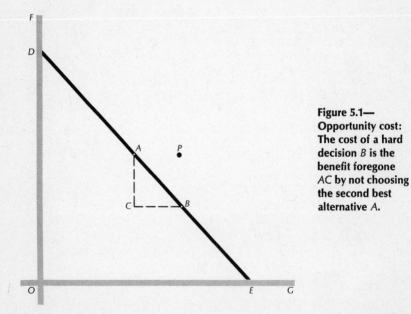

Figure 5.1—Opportunity cost: The cost of a hard decision B is the benefit foregone AC by not choosing the second best alternative A.

And in an economy where some resources are unemployed (some of the inputs unused during the given time period) few of both goods may be produced.

The possible bills of outputs are all shown on Figure 5.1. Any point inside or on the triangle ODE is *feasible*. that is, the bundle of amounts of F and G represented by that point can actually be turned out by the production system during the time period. Thus points *O, D, C,* and *A* represent feasible bills of outputs, but point *P* is infeasible. In Figure 5.1 let us compare two points on the line *DE,* such as *A* and *B.* Suppose the economy were to move from *A* to *B,* that is to change its production pattern from the bundle of goods represented by *A* to the bundle of goods represented by *B.* The incentive to do this is the additional consumer goods which would then be produced, an amount represented on the diagram by the distance *CB.* However, the diagram tells us that we cannot get more consumer goods without getting along with fewer factories. The distance *AC* tells us how many fewer factories we get when we go to *B.*

Points *A* and *B* represent economic alternatives available to the economy and the distance *AC* the opportunity cost of moving from *A* to *B.*

▶   *Opportunity cost measures the value of the opportunities forgone by choosing one alternative rather than another.*

If the economy in fact *does* move from *A* to *B* it is presumably because the gains from the move, the additional consumer goods, are considered to be greater than the opportunity cost.

Notice that the steepness of the line *DE* measures the relative costs and gains from moving between two points. For example, if it were steeper the distance *BC* in the triangle *ABC* would be shorter. The gains from moving from *A* to *B* would be less, and so perhaps the move would not occur. *DE* is called the *transformation line* because when we move from one point to another on it we are in effect transforming some of one good into another. When we move from *A* to *B,* we transform *AC* of factories into *BC* of consumer goods on our final bill of goods produced during the time period.

DE has been drawn on a straight line in Figure 5.1. Is it reasonable to assume that the transformation line should be straight? Probably over a certain range of alternatives it often *is* linear or pretty nearly so. However, it seems likely that this is not always so. Figure 5.2 shows a transformation line which is concave, when looked at from the origin *O.* The reason for thinking it will have this shape can be seen by looking at the three pairs of alternatives drawn in Figure 5.2. The distance *BC, B'C',* and *B"C"* are all equal; that is, in each move the economy gains the same amount of consumer goods. However, *A'C'* is smaller than *AC* and *AC* is smaller than *A"C"*; that, is in moving from *A'* to *B'* the opportunity cost in terms of factories is less than in moving from *A* to *B,* while the latter move has a smaller opportunity cost than the move from *A"* to *B".* The reason for these differences lies in relative amounts of the two goods that are being

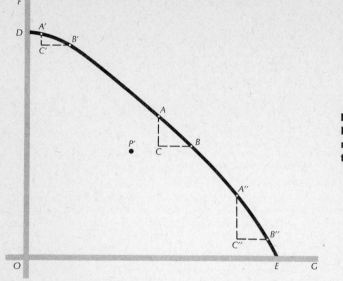

**Figure 5.2—
Diminishing
marginal rate of
transformation.**

produced in each case. At *A'* a great many factories are being produced relative to consumer goods. We are near capacity production
of factories so that bottlenecks and extra costs are likely to be
incurred. At this high-cost rate of production of factories we can
release quite a few productive services by reducing factory production only a little bit. This is what the slope of *DE* in the vicinity of *A'*
tells us. Just the opposite is the case at *A"*, where a relatively large
amount of consumer goods and few factories are being produced.
To produce still more consumer goods requires a large sacrifice in
terms of factories forgone.

Earlier we spoke of the rate of transformation of factories into
consumer goods. Now we see that this rate of transformation may be
different at different points along the transformation line *DE*. To
make sure we are aware of this possibility, we speak of the *marginal* rate of transformation of one good into another.

►   *For example, the marginal rate of transformation of factories
into consumer goods is the number of factories we must
give up at some given point in order to get a small increase
in the amount of consumer goods produced.*

We must think in terms of small increases because, when the
transformation line is curved, the number of factories that must be
given up to get a given increase in consumer goods varies continuously as the economy moves along the line.

Before leaving the transformation line, we may ask one last question: What is the opportunity cost of moving from *P'* to *A*? The

answer is that the opportunity cost is zero. No scarce or valuable goods are given up when we make this move. The economy gets more of both factories and consumer goods.

Now let us think of another production system, one which con- **Inputs and** tains both inputs and outputs. We are interested in describing the **Outputs** possible transformations of inputs into outputs. This time we can ignore inefficient transformations and deal only with the maximum output possible with each given amount of input. One possible relation between input and output:

> ► *Constant returns to scale occur when increasing all inputs in some proportion makes possible an increase in outputs in that same proportion.*

Constant returns to scale means for example that if the amount of all inputs is doubled then the outputs will also be doubled if only efficient transformations are considered.

> ► ► *All production transformations must exhibit constant returns to scale, provided only that the factors are divisible.*

This is, one way to double output is to reproduce the production system; since production in the new system is carried out in the same way as in the old, inputs and outputs are exactly doubled. An output increase by 10 per cent could yield constant returns by producing an "eleventh" production system just like each of the "first ten." This is possible, provided the first production system can really be divided up into ten identical production systems each producing a tenth of the outputs with a tenth of each input. Of course this is not always possible in practice, but the constant-returns case is often a close enough approximation to reality, especially over longer time periods, to be useful in practical work.

Now let us consider a case in which proportionate increase of all inputs is not possible. A factory cannot be expanded within the production period, say, or a farmer cannot expand the acreage he plants. However, though some inputs are fixed in amount, others are variable—for example, the amount of labor used or the amount of fertilizer applied to the land. We can define

> ► *The marginal product, which is the additional output resulting from a small increase in the use of some input, other inputs being held constant.*

This concept makes it possible to state simply some fundamental properties of production technologies and their implications for resource analysis. Perhaps the most important of these is the principle of diminishing marginal returns.

►► *All factors of production exhibit diminishing marginal returns; that is, when some factors are held fixed and the amount of another factor is increased, beyond some point the marginal product of that factor begins to decline.*

This is one of those propositions about the real world that seem almost trivial but are really quite fundamental. If diminishing returns did not set in eventually it would be possible, for example, to grow the entire world's food supply on a single acre of land simply by increasing the amount of labor applied to it. Each additional laborer would by definition contribute at least as much of an increase in output as the one before. Consequently workers could be shifted from other plots of land to this one without reducing output. We observe nothing like this actually happening in practice and so accept diminishing returns. In fact diminishing returns generally set in early enough in the course of expansion of individual factors that it is taken as the norm. In the analysis that follows we will be dealing with situations in which diminishing returns are already operating.

Circular Flow and Production

Suppose we think of the economy as consisting of only two kinds of decision makers: households and businesses. Since production is carried out by businesses, we will lump all businesses together and call them the production system. We also lump households together in a single group. What we are interested in is the interactions between the production system and households. Since we are not interested in interactions *among* households or *among* businesses, we simply ignore them, or rather we assume that these latter interactions have no effect on the over-all level of economic activity.

How do households and the production system interact? In the first place households provide both labor and capital services to business. In return for this they receive money payments from business. With the money thus received households buy consumer goods and services from business, so that there is a flow of goods from business to households and a flow of money in the opposite direction. This process is shown in Figure 5.3. Notice that there is a circular flow of goods and services in one direction and an opposite flow of money. Since markets are used for all these transactions, the value of the goods flowing in either pipeline must exactly equal the opposite flow of money in the corresponding pipeline.

Must the flow in the upper pipelines be equal to the flow in the lower ones? This question is equivalent to the following one: Can one of the sectors absorb more than it "emits," or vice versa? Turning to the business sector, it appears that the answer is "yes." It could absorb additional services but put the products into inventories instead of selling them to consumers. The same would seem to be true

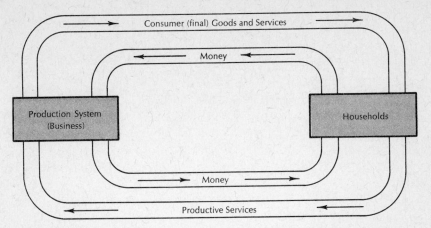

Figure 5.3—The circular flow of goods and productive services and of money.

of the consumer sector, which could buy more or fewer goods by spending more or less than it earns, rather than varying the amount of services it supplies to business.

In fact the above answers are wrong, as is suggested by our earlier definition of final goods. We are interested in productive activity that is carried out in the current period and results in final goods. Consequently all the labor and capital services flowing through the lower pipe must be used during the current period. The results of their use flow out of the production system through the upper pipe, and only those final goods produced during the current period are included. Thus inventories as part of final demand flow out and are in effect transferred to households in the diagram.

► *Thus the value of the flow into the production system of factors of production during the time period must equal the value of the flow out of the production system of final goods during that same period.*

Notice that this is a definition rather than a proposition. We define economic flows this way because this mode of analysis is used to evaluate current-period economic activity. Hence it is important to include only activities that are carried out during the period. In the input-output model, to which we now turn, the same assumption is made about the relation between factors of production and final demands.

Our model will contain two goods which can serve both as final and as intermediate goods, and one factor of production. Our two goods and the industries that produce them will be numbered 1 and 2 and might stand for steel and plastics respectively, each of which may be used either in further processing or turned over to the con-

The Input-Output Model of Production

sumer or investor (factory-builder) for final consumption. The total amount of each good produced during the production period will be denoted x_1 and x_2 respectively. The total amount flowing out of the production system into final demand will be y_1 and y_2. Thus, $(x_1 - y_1)$ is the amount of the first good (steel) that is used as an intermediate good. Finally our factor of production will be labor but its amount will be assigned the letter f to suggest that it might be any of a number of different factors of production. f is a fixed amount, say 20,000,000 man-years, implying that our production period is so short that we do not add significantly to the labor force during it (or more likely that we know in advance approximately how much labor will be available). The amount of labor assigned to each industry is represented by f_1 and f_2.

Each industry must use some labor in producing x_1 and x_2, the gross outputs as we call them. In addition they may use some steel as an input in order to produce steel as an output. For example, under the older open-hearth process scrap steel was a very important input, though with the new oxygen converters it has become relatively unimportant. And we will assume that the steel industry also uses some plastics in its production processes—perhaps as special clothing for some of the workers. To make our model as general as possible we will assume that each industry uses some of each industry's output as an input to its own production process.

▶   *In an input-output model gross outputs are assumed to be proportional to inputs.*

Behind this definition lie two assumptions: that inputs are used efficiently, and that there are constant returns to scale within the model. The latter means that if all inputs to an industry are doubled output will double. The former means that strict proportionality will prevail, so that an industry will never double the amount of one input and treble that of another. If it did output could only double and some of the input that was trebled would be wasted. We will also assume that no inputs are used if no output is obtained.

Our model seems to be ignoring capital. In a sense this is true. Implicitly it is assumed that the factories and the land needed to produce the goods are already there and there will be no capacity bottlenecks to prevent us from achieving various mixes of output. What will keep us from producing infinite amounts of goods is the labor constraint. Each industry uses labor, and there is only a limited amount of it available. This of course is a serious deviation from reality, but we must begin with a simple description of reality. Later we can explore some of the implications of a more complex world. This one is complex enough to possess some interesting properties and is sufficiently close to the real world to be a useful device for the practical analysis of certain real-world situations.

Table 5.1—Technical coefficients for industry

Inputs from	Industry 1	Industry 2
Industry 1	a_{11}	a_{12}
Industry 2	a_{21}	a_{22}
Factor f	a_{f1}	a_{f2}

Table 5.1 lists our technical coefficients of production. They tell us how much of each input is needed to produce a unit of gross output in each industry. Thus a_{21} tells us how many tons of good 2 plastics) will be needed to produce a ton of good 1 (steel), a_{f2} tells us how many man-hours of labor will be needed to produce a ton of plastics, and so on. These coefficients are fixed in value; that is, no matter how much is actually being produced it will take the same additional amount of each input to produce an additional unit of output. Armed with these we can now write balances of sources and uses for each good.

Source		Uses:			
Production		Intermediate		Final	
x_1	$=$	$a_{11}x_1 + a_{12}x_2$	$+$	y_1	(1)
x_2	$=$	$a_{21}x_1 + a_{22}x_2$	$+$	y_2	(2)

Equation (1) tells us that our sole source of good 1 during the production period is actual production. It can be used partly to produce goods 1 and 2 and be partly transferred to final uses for consumption, investment, or (net) exports. Our efficiency assumption insures that sources and uses balance. We could not produce less of a good than will be assigned to intermediate and final demand because this would violate our assumptions about the processes of production. We will not produce more, for that would be wasteful, giving us more than the model tells us is needed. Note that the individual products under intermediate uses give us the amounts required in each intermediate use. Thus if we are going to produce x_2 units of plastics and it takes a_{12} tons of steel to produce a ton of plastics, then the plastics industry requires $a_{12}x_2$ units of steel as an intermediate input.

Notice that each of our letters stands for a number. We could as well have put specific numbers in but by using letters we achieve greater generality. Nevertheless there are some restrictions on just what values the x can be substituted for if the model is to make any sense. Thus we do not use negative amounts of goods as inputs in producing other goods, so the coefficient of production cannot be negative in sign.

There is one additional balance that must be included—the labor balance:

$$a_{f1}x_1 + a_{f2}x_2 = f.$$

This tells us that all labor is used up in producing one good or the other.

Now we are in a position to draw our input-output model on a diagram. The valuable products of the production system are the final goods. Intermediate goods are only a means to an end and so are not intrinsically valuable. And labor, the factor of production, is simply to be used up—that is, we assume that its most valuable alternative uses are in production not in idleness. Therefore we will plot final demands on our diagram with the amount of y_1 on the horizontal axis and y_2 on the vertical axis as in Figure 5.4. How much final demand can we get? To answer this let us start with two unusually simple but unrealistic situations. In the first it is decided to produce none of good 2 whatsoever. All labor is to be used up in the production of

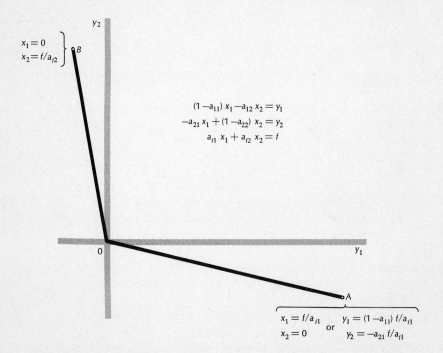

$$(1 - a_{11}) x_1 - a_{12} x_2 = y_1$$
$$-a_{21} x_1 + (1 - a_{22}) x_2 = y_2$$
$$a_{f1} x_1 + a_{f2} x_2 = f$$

$x_1 = 0$
$x_2 = f/a_{f2}$

$$x_1 = f/a_{f1} \quad \text{or} \quad y_1 = (1 - a_{11}) f/a_{f1}$$
$$x_2 = 0 \qquad\qquad y_2 = -a_{21} f/a_{f1}$$

Figure 5.4—Input-output: The effect on final demand of using all of the factor f in industry 1 (point A) or all of it in industry 2 (point B).

good 1. How much final demand will result? We know that it takes a_{f1} units of labor to produce a unit of gross output, of x_1. Therefore we get f/a_{f1} units of x_1 if we use all our available labor in industry 1. This is not all final demand, however, since part of x_1 is used up in producing good 1. So we must deduct this amount, which is $a_{11}x_1$. From our balancing equation, remembering that $x_2 = 0$, we see that $y_1 = x_1 - a_{11}x_1$, which checks the argument. This tells us how far out to the right we can get on Figure 5.4.

Now we turn to the vertical axis. We will be producing none of good 2; however, industry 1 uses good 2 in production. Solving our second balancing equation on the assumption that $x_2 = 0$ gives us $y_2 = -a_{21}x_1$. Since both a_{21} and x_1 are known to be positive, this means that y_2 must be negative in sign. But this is reasonable enough. We need some of good 2 but are not going to be producing any of it during the production period. Hence we must draw down existing stocks of the good, inventories left over from previous production periods. And this is precisely the meaning of a negative y_2. Changes in inventories are a part of investment, which is a part of final demand, from our previous definition. This, finally, gives us point A on the diagram. Given that there are stocks of good 2 available, this represents a point that can actually be achieved under our assumed conditions of production and availability of labor and good 2.

An exactly similar argument will give us point B in Figure 5.4. This is the maximum amount of y_2 that can be delivered by the production system, given that all labor is allocated to industry 2 and that there are sufficient stocks of good 1 on hand to make this level of production of industry 2 feasible.

Many other combinations of final goods are also possible. Given points A and B it is now easy to fill in the rest. We need only go back to our proportionality assumption. This tells us that a unit of labor transferred from industry 2 to industry 1 will produce the same reduction in final demand, y_1, and increase in final demand, y_2, regardless of how much is being produced at the moment. This is the same thing as saying that the opportunity cost of additional units of good 2 in terms of units of good 1 that must be forgone is constant over the range of production possibilities. Our transformation line is straight. Since we already have identified two points on it we can draw it in immediately. AB represents the production possibilities for our simple production system.[3]

In drawing Figure 5.5 the connection between a factor of produc-

<hr>

3. We have not mentioned the adjustments that the existence of intermediate goods requires when labor is reallocated. However, our proportionality assumption takes care of this, too. Regardless of what mix of goods 1 and 2 is presently being produced, the same adjustment of intermediate goods must take place along with the labor reallocation.

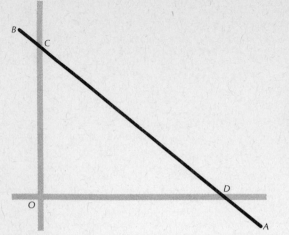

Figure 5.5—A transformation line for the input-output model.

tion and final demands in a complex production system has been shown. The final picture shows the range of efficient alternatives open to the users of that system. A few comments on its properties are now in order.

1. A major feature of input-output models is that they provide a quantitative evaluation of the effects of interdependence. The complex ways in which goods are related to one another in production are organized systematically and measured. Thus an aspect of reality that seems bewildering in its interactions becomes intelligible.

2. Using input-output, alternative bills of goods can be evaluated as to their cost. The development of a production possibilities line has already shown us this possibility. The slope of AB (or CD, taking account of the fact that we will rarely be relying wholly on previous stocks of goods for inputs) gives us the opportunity cost of increasing the amount of final demand of good 1 or of good 2.

3. Such a model can also be used to estimate the factor requirements for a given bill of goods. By starting with a prescribed bill of final demands and reversing the procedure of the last few pages we can calculate how much of some factor of production will be required to produce that bill of goods. As long as we have a set of factor coefficients (like a_{f1} and a_{f2}) we can do this, one after another, for any number of such factors.

4. In practical use any number of industries may be used in the model, without any significant change in the structure of the model. A recent U.S. model has eighty sectors, and a great many countries have constructed models having 20–50 sectors. Regional models are also possible. For example, the states of California and Utah have input-output models for their state economies, which can be put to similar uses as the national models.

5. One of the most important uses of these models is in planning economic development. The planners have some idea as to how final demands will be changed five years hence. By using an input-output model they can find out how much capacity will be needed in each industry if those final demands are to be realized. In this case it is the x_1 and x_2 of our model, the gross outputs, that answer their question. A related use is for studying the impact of mobilization for war. A model containing several hundred sectors was constructed for the United States in the late 1940s with this end in view.

6. It should be remembered that input-output is a model of reality, not reality itself. Consequently the results of an analysis using input-output will not be very accurate if the economy does not look much like the model—that is, if the assumptions are not fairly close to reality. If doubling inputs more than doubles output or if the coefficients are wrong or change substantially over the period of analysis, the results may deviate substantially from reality.[4]

7. Finally, we have said nothing about how our economy is organized. We will return to this question and its implications for models of production in Chapter 10. Our purpose in this section has been to show one way in which the production system can be analyzed so as to display for a decision maker the kinds of alternatives that are *technologically* possible for the economy. Until we know more about how decisions are actually taken and how decision makers are organized we are not able to say anything about which alternatives will be taken, not even whether they will be efficient.

Technologically Determined Prices

In Figure 5.6 we have drawn again the transformation line *TT* and so are returning to the production system in which the marginal rate of transformation is declining. Suppose *TT* represents the possibilities open to a businessman. His costs are fixed, since the amount of inputs available to him is fixed. If he is to maximize profits then he will have to find that combination of outputs which produces the maximum revenue. We can draw in a budget line, such as was used in Chapter 4 to discuss consumption. This line, *BB,* shows the relative price of the two outputs by means of its slope, just as it did in Chapter 4. An outward shift in the line means an increase in the total value of each bundle of goods represented by points on the line. Thus revenue to the firm will be maximized at a point still touching *TT*. The combination of outputs represented by point *A* in Figure 5.6 is thus a feasible bill of outputs and provides the maximum revenue to the firm. It is the profit maximizing bill of outputs under our assumptions.

4. Note the extreme version of diminishing marginal returns assumed by input-output analysis. If the other inputs are held fixed and one input is increased, the marginal product is zero, and this is true for every input in every industry. The only efficient combinations of inputs for an industry are proportional to each other.

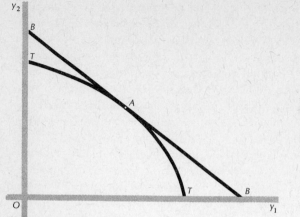

**Figure 5.6—
Opportunity cost
and relative prices.**

Notice that very small movements along the transformation line are almost equivalent to movements along the budget line. The slopes are so nearly identical that for such small movements we can ignore the difference. This leads us to an important conclusion:

►► *At the profit-maximizing point the relative prices of the outputs are equal to the opportunity cost (marginal rate of
transformation).*

That is, prices provide a measure of the value forgone by producing a little more of one good and a little less of another. Opportunity cost was described earlier as a strictly technological concept, related to the technical limitations on transformations of goods. The prices however are economically determined in the market place. Thus we see how in equilibrium technological and economic factors become closely linked. Note also that even if no market existed opportunity cost can be given an economic interpretation. So long as both outputs are valued by some decision maker, the (technological) opportunity cost tells him something about the terms on which alternatives are available to him. Thus he may use opportunity costs in the same way in which he would have used market prices, had they been available to him, in comparing the various courses of action open to him.

Turn back now to Figure 5.5, which is the transformation line derived from the input-output model. *CD* therefore displays the alternative bills of final goods available to an economy. But unlike *TT* in Figure 5.6, *CD* is a straight line. Thus opportunity cost is constant and does not depend on the particular bill of goods chosen (provided of course that it is efficient and uses all of the available scarce factor). This means that for the input-output model a shift in demand which leads to a new bill of final goods will not change the relative prices of those goods, since (unlike *TT* in Figure 5.6) all budget lines tangent to *CD* will be coincident with it.[5] This is a consequence of the special technological assumptions of the model. It fits the cost of production theories of value, such as those of classical and Marxian economics, since it leads to the conclusion that relative values (prices) are strictly determined by the conditions of production. While the assumption is useful for many purposes it does overstate the connections between technology and price. The looser framework suggested by Figure 5.6, in which changes in demand, as reflected in the slope of the budget line, can change relative prices, is preferred in most applied and theoretical work.

5. At the corners *C* and *D* this is not true, but we can ignore them on the assumption that all the goods we are interested in are actually produced.

6

The Enterprise

The enterprise, the basic production-decision unit in the economy, is capable of carrying out some limited set of transformations of goods and services. The enterprise decision maker, which we might as well call the businessman since we are dealing with a market economy, must know the properties of the alternatives in his production system. However, his choice of alternatives is not determined by technological conditions alone. In this chapter we look at the way in which economic and technological aspects are combined in alternatives and how the businessman reacts. We will begin by assuming that decisions are being taken with respect to a single time period and that what happens outside that time period is irrelevant to the decisions.

Revenue   In the preceding chapter opportunity cost was defined as the benefit forgone by not choosing some other alternative. The opportunity cost of going to the movies tonight may be the benefit forgone by not going to the opera. Direct money costs do not always measure opportunity cost for businessmen. For example, consider a man who has saved some money and is considering buying a shop and running it himself. The opportunity cost of buying the shop includes not only the benefits from alternative uses of the money he would have to spend to buy the shop, but also the wages he would forgo by being his own boss rather than continuing in his present job. However, the market usually puts a price on the costs that are relevant for most business decisions. For example, our potential shop-keeper can easily calculate the wages he would earn and the things he could buy with the purchase price of the store and take account of these in making his decision. So, bearing in mind what we mean by costs, let us assume that we can always find a satisfactory money measure of them in what follows.

Let us now turn to revenue, the money receipts of a firm from sell-ing its goods and services. We will be working with three revenue concepts:

► *Total revenue: the total amount of money receipts from the sale of some given amount of goods.*

► *Average revenue: the total revenue divided by the number of units of the good sold.*

► *Marginal revenue: the amount by which total revenue in-creases when one more unit of the good is sold.*

Here is a perhaps unexpected relationship involving these concepts:

►► *Average revenue equals price.*

Average revenue tells how much, on the average, the firm receives from the sale of each unit of its product. In Chapter 3 we learned that on a market all units of a good tend to be sold at a single price. But this price must be the average revenue, since price times quantity equals total revenue, and so does average revenue times (the same) quantity. Therefore

►► *A demand curve is also an average-revenue curve, showing at the same time the price and the average revenue asso-ciated with the sale of varying quantities of the good.*

Another relationship of interest to us is that between marginal and average revenue. We have seen that it is almost universally true that the amount demanded tends to increase with a fall in price. On a diagram like Figure 6.1b this is shown by the *AR* line which slopes downward to the right.

►► *For downward-sloping demand curves, marginal revenue is always less than average revenue.*

To see why this is true, let us suppose that a firm is selling *OB* goods at price *BE*, as shown in Figure 6.1b. The manager is trying to decide whether to lower price by a small amount. He knows that if

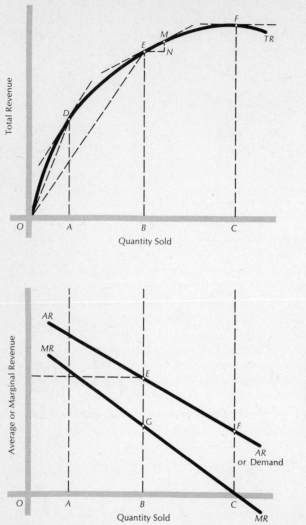

**Figure 6.1a,b—
Total, average, and
marginal revenue.**

he does he will sell, say, an additional unit and that this in itself will
increase his revenue by a little bit less than the going price *BE*. However, since all units must be sold at a single price, he will also have
to sell the goods *OB* at a new lower price and this will reduce his
total revenue somewhat. The net result of these two factors is an
increase in total revenue of substantially less than the new price of
the good and, if demand is inelastic, it may actually lead to a reduction in total revenue. This net effect is *BG*, the marginal revenue from
an additional sale.

These relationships can also be illustrated in a different kind of diagram. In Figure 6.1a the total revenue is plotted in the vertical direction. Any point like *E* on the *TR* line gives two numbers: the amount sold (equal to *OB*) and the total revenue received (equal to *BE*). On this diagram

▶ *Average revenue at any point like E is measured by the steepness of the line from the point E to the origin (that is, by the steepness of OE);*

▶ *Marginal revenue is measured by the steepness of the line tangent to the total revenue line at the given point (for example the dashed line that just touches TR at E).*

The steepness of *OE* depends on the ratio of *BE* to *OB*; the first of these measures total revenue, the second quantity sold. Their quotient, by definition, is average revenue. The marginal relationship can be seen from the small triangle at *E*. *MN* measures (roughly) the increase in total revenue associated with an increase in sales of *EN* units. This is, from our definition, marginal revenue, and the ratio (or quotient) of the two gives us the steepness of the tangent line at *E*. By comparing the appropriate lines at points *D* and *E* in Figure 6.1a, we can easily verify that at both points the marginal-revenue (tangent) line is less steep than the average-revenue (ray through the origin) line. So marginal revenue is less than average revenue, as is the case for the corresponding sales points in Figure 6.1b.

The reader can check his understanding to this point by looking at point *F* on both panels of Figure 6.1. What does marginal revenue equal at sales level *OC* on each diagram? You should get the same answer on both diagrams. Also, our profit-maximizing manager is not interested in points beyond (to the right of) *OC*. Why not? And finally: how can you find total revenue on Figure 6.1b?

We turn now to a look at the way costs vary as the level of output **Cost** of the product is changed. The task is made much easier because similar concepts hold in the case of both cost and revenue. We have three parallel concepts:

▶ *Total cost: the total amount of money costs required to produce some given amount of goods (assuming that money costs are a good measure of opportunity cost).*

▶ *Average cost: the total cost divided by the number of units of the good produced. This is sometimes called unit cost.*

▶ *Marginal cost: the amount by which total cost increases when one more unit of the good is produced.*

There are, of course, parallel relationships among these concepts,

too, but they are not the same as those for the revenue concepts because the shapes of the curves relating them to quantity produced
are different. It is widely true that average cost curves are dish-shaped,
as shown in Figure 6.2b. When an enterprise is initially designed, it

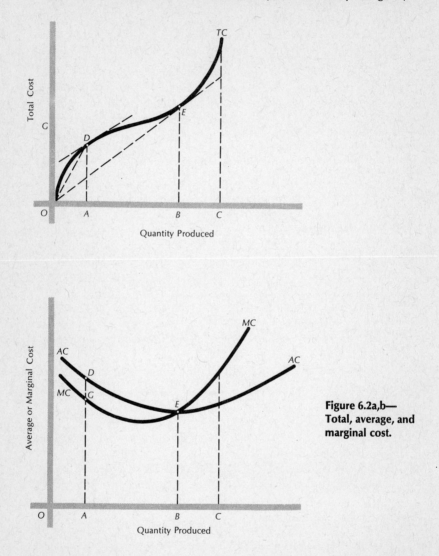

**Figure 6.2a,b—
Total, average, and
marginal cost.**

is usually expected that it will be operating most of the time in the
general area of output *OB* of Figure 6.2b, at which point average costs
are at a minimum. At lower levels of operation average costs are
likely to be higher for several reasons. There are some costs that
must be incurred if any output at all is to be had, such as the cost of
the land and the factory building. When output is low the average

of these costs will be rather high, pulling the average cost curve up. These are called:

▶ *Fixed costs, which are costs that do not vary with short-run changes in the level of output.*

A second reason is that some factors of production are lumpy or indivisible. You cannot have less than one lathe and still get lathe services, so your unit costs will be high unless operation is at the capacity level of at least one lathe. A third reason is organizational. If a factory is operating at well below its designed level, inefficiencies result simply from the fact that you are doing many things differently than was planned, as when some workers have to double at jobs that would be distinct specialties at normal levels of operation.

At levels of operation well above *OB*, average costs again are likely to rise. Older stand-by equipment may have to be put into operation and less efficient workers hired or existing staff paid overtime. Inefficiencies are likely to result from crowding and bottlenecks.

Of course the average-cost curve varies widely in shape from one factory to the next. In many the dish may be flat over a wide range, indicating that average costs are roughly constant except for extreme variations of output levels. In others the rate of operation of the factory may be quite inflexible and shutdown and starting up costs quite high, so that the shape is more like a "V." We will stick to the curved-dish shape in our diagrams because that is the most convenient way to display relationships.

The shape of the total cost curve of Figure 6.2a reflects the dish shape of the average-cost curve of Figure 6.2b. As with the total revenue diagram, the marginal and average cost associated with a given level of production is equal to the slopes or steepness of the tangent and ray through the origin respectively. Notice from the two figures that:

▶ ▶ *Marginal cost is below average cost when the latter is falling and above average cost when the latter is rising.*

This is a generalization of the relation between marginal and average revenue. In working with revenue concepts, we considered only falling average revenue, since this is the only likely situation. But rising average cost is very likely and so we add a new clause to the corresponding statement for cost analysis. The reason for this relationship is easy to see. Think, for example, of output *OA* in Figure 6.2b. Average cost is *AD*, marginal cost the smaller amount, *AG*. If when an additional unit is produced, the extra total cost is less than average, this will have a tendency to pull average cost down; and vice versa for a marginal cost higher than average cost (as at output *OC*). The reader should verify that this is also true in Figure 6.2a.

▶ ▶ *Marginal cost equals average cost at the output level at which average cost is a minimum.*

This output level is *OB* on both panels of Figure 6.2, and both figures verify the relationship. The reason this is true can best be seen by referring back to our last relationship. If marginal cost is below average cost, it is pulling the latter up. What if marginal cost is not pulling in either direction? Then, of course, it is equal to average cost. At the minimum average cost point this happens because only there is average cost flat briefly while it is changing directions. This will become even more apparent if average cost has a flattened-dish shape. Then over the range, constant average cost and marginal and average costs must be equal; for if they were not, average cost would be pulled either up or down.

The Profit-Maximizing Firm

Many firms have other goals than the making of profits. Some will be willing to pay a price in profits in order to increase their share of the market. Others may simply be content with a "reasonable" return on investment and make little effort to better the level of performance deemed acceptable by the firm's leadership; such firms are perhaps substituting leisure for the owners and less intensive performance by employees for profits. But profits are such an important element in every firm's goals that it is probably not such a gross oversimplification to assume that this is all they want. Perhaps the central importance of profits is most decisively suggested by the experience of countries that have tried to use other criteria in running industry. The Communist countries of Eastern Europe, including the Soviet Union, have recently been returning to a much increased use of profits as an aid to enterprise decision making. Through the study of price theory we can get some idea as to why profits are so useful and important.

Figure 6.3a imposes a total-cost and total-revenue curve on the same diagram. This can be done because cost and revenue are measured in the same units, dollars, and output sold and produced are also both measured in terms of the physical units of the good, such as pounds or dozens. At what point will a profit-maximizing manager choose to operate his production establishment? Profits are the difference between revenue and cost. Where that difference is greatest, profits are greatest. Clearly this is at output level *OQ*, where the vertical difference between *TC* and *TR* is greatest, for obvious reasons, given that *TR* is above *TC*. An interesting property of this output level is the following:

▶ ▶ *Marginal cost equals marginal revenue at the profit-maximizing output level.*

To see why this should be true, think of an output level less than

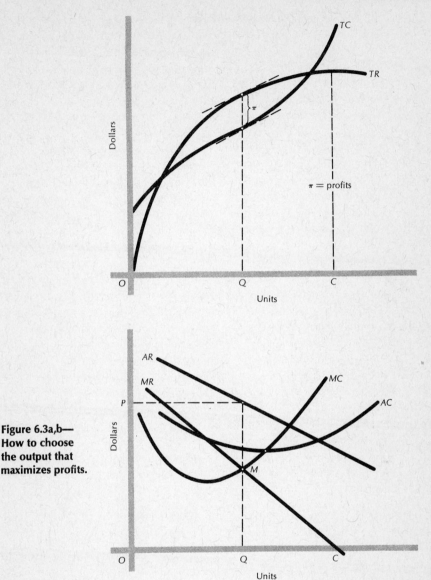

**Figure 6.3a,b—
How to choose
the output that
maximizes profits.**

OQ. Here it is seen from the diagram that marginal revenue is greater than marginal cost, which is itself a consequence of the assumed shapes of the revenue and cost curves. The meaning of this difference is that if production and sales are increased by one unit, total revenue will increase by more than total cost. But this is another way of saying that more output means increased profits, so the manager would shift his output level up toward OQ. Now consider the output level above OQ. Here marginal cost is greater than marginal revenue. An increase in output will increase total cost by more than total revenue and so decrease profits. Therefore the manager will shift his output level down toward OQ. Only at OQ can he find no profitable movement in either direction. Thus armed with quantitative information about the way cost and revenue vary with output, the manager has a simple criterion for deciding at what level to produce: choose that level of output at which marginal cost equals marginal revenue.

In analyzing markets, we were able to obtain quite a bit of information about their operation by studying the effects of shifts in supply and demand curves. The same approach can be used in looking at our profit-maximizing managers. Suppose, for example, that demand for the product increased. Remembering that the average revenue curve is also a demand curve, this means that the AR line in Figure 6.3b shifts up and out to the right. Naturally the marginal-revenue curve goes along with it, shifting up and to the right also. Marginal revenue and marginal cost will then be equal at some point farther out on the marginal cost curve. This means that our manager will sell more goods than OQ at a higher price than OP. Alternatively, costs might increase, say as a result of higher wages. This increase shifts the average- and marginal-cost curves up without affecting demand significantly. Marginal cost will equal marginal revenue farther back to the left on the marginal-revenue curve. The result will be less production than OQ at a higher price than OP. The study of shifts of this kind is very useful in analyzing the effects of trade unions on wage rates and employment levels and in many other economic analyses.

Let us now turn to a slightly more complicated assumption about time. There are now two time periods, which we call the short and the long run.

▶ *Variable costs are those that can vary with the level of output during some given time period. Fixed costs are those that cannot.*

▶ *In the long run all costs are variable. The short run is a time period during which some costs are fixed.*

Naturally, total variable costs increase as the level of output increases. Of course, for any given time period, all costs are either variable or fixed, and all fixed costs are variable in the long run.

In the long run all costs are variable because the businessman or potential businessman has the option of not going into business or of choosing any one of the possible different plant sizes which engineers can design. Big plants require more land, bigger buildings, more janitorial and security services, and so forth, than small ones. But once the decision as to plant size has been made and the new plant is in operation, these costs become fixed over periods of time shorter than the economic life of the plant. Thus the short run may be defined as the period of time over which the size of the plant is taken as given and decisions relate only to the level of operation of these existing facilities. Of course the calendar length of the short run varies from business to business. For the apple peddler or small shopkeeper the short run may be very short indeed, since the facilities needed to expand the capacity of the operation may be readily at hand (the cart shop with its various sized carts ready to be pushed off the salesroom floor or the vacant shops, larger and smaller, which dot the neighborhood). For a railroad or electric power company the short run may be a decade or even more for some decisions. Though the short and long runs are highly variable in their temporal implications, nevertheless for any given decision it is fairly easy to make the distinction.

These two concepts will now be used to show an important difference between the behavior of our profit-maximizing businessman in the short run and in the long run. In the latter case, clearly no businessman will go into business unless he expects to make a profit. Thus if the total cost curve of Figure 6.3a lay above the total revenue curve at every output, and these curves described expected costs and revenues over the long run, there would be no new firms established in that industry. However, this is not true in the short run. To see why not, let us begin with a somewhat different relationship:

▶ ▶   *A change in fixed cost has no effect on the short-run behavior of a profit-maximizing firm.*

Going back to Figure 6.2a, we see that at zero output total cost is zero. This implies that there are no fixed costs, since, for example, rent would have to be paid in the short run even though no output was being produced. (Note that from the concept of opportunity cost this statement is true even if the firm owns its own land. Why?) Indeed we may interpret this diagram as showing a long-run total cost curve. But suppose that it is treated as a short-run diagram. Then plainly we have left fixed costs out of account and this curve shows only total variable costs. How do we put fixed costs in? Well, if fixed costs do not vary with output, at each level of output total cost should be higher by exactly the amount of fixed costs, say $10,000. On the diagram this means a shift of the total cost curve straight up, without any change in its shape. These two total cost curves are shown in Figure 6.4. But if the curve shifts straight up, then there is no change in its slope at any point. Hence marginal cost remains constant when

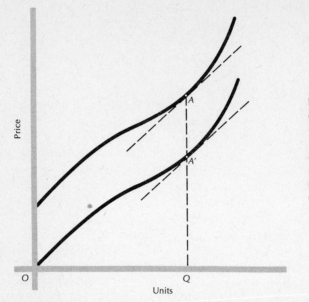

Figure 6.4—A change in fixed cost does not change marginal cost and so does not affect the short-run output decision.

fixed cost changes. Since nothing has happened to revenue, the marginal-revenue curve is also unchanged and so the equilibrium point is the same as before, and our assertion is true. Any change in fixed costs simply shifts the total cost curve straight up or down and does not affect marginal cost. The additional cost of increasing output by a unit is the same after the change in fixed cost as it was before at every level of output.

Now we can state an addition to our manager's rule for short-run operation:

►► *The profit-maximizing firm will operate at the point where marginal cost equals marginal revenue, even though this means taking losses, provided only that total variable costs are covered. If they are not covered, he will shut down.*

The fixed costs are sunk costs; that is, nothing can be done to change them in the short run. If the manager finds that at the marginal-revenue-equals-marginal-cost point his total revenue is less than total cost but greater than total variable cost, he will not shut down because by operating he is running smaller losses. He can at least pay some of his fixed cost out of the revenue left over when variable cost has been paid. If he shut down he would have no revenue to use to pay anything.

Time, Risk, and Information A businessman is often uncertain as to what things will be like in the next period. At the same time he has a very complicated series of decisions to make which will affect his profits both this period and next. He will typically be buying and selling in many markets, will have to bear in mind his production system alternatives, and must keep the organization functioning smoothly. Whatever the size of his business he will probably want to simplify many of the decisions so as to be able to give adequate attention to the most important ones. Often this involves the specialization of information used by any one businessman and the shifting of risks from one business to another.

Let us look very briefly at some kinds of risk shifting commonly practiced by enterprises. Insurance is an almost universally adopted form. Insurance for enterprises has similar properties to those of household insurance. The enterprise is in effect choosing a smaller level of profits with certainty rather than a gamble (see chapter 4). Insurance is available to enterprises only for a limited range of risks, however. Only those risks which the insurance companies can evaluate with confidence, and for which policies can be sold in quantity are likely to be insurable. Such things as fire and theft are generally insurable, while war and flood insurance are much more difficult to obtain. A major reason for this is that the latter risks are not independent of one another. The fact that one firm has been hit by war or flood changes the odds that another firm will be so hit.

Another method of risk shifting is by forward-sale contracts. For example a contractor wins a bid to carry out a construction project next period. He is not sure what the prices of some of the goods and services, say painting, will be next period but has based his bid on a current estimate of the future prices. In order to avoid risk himself he immediately lets subcontracts at fixed prices for these services.

By contracting in advance the businessman has avoided the risk of an unfavorable price change. But he is not secure against the risk of a favorable change: in our example if the price of painting services is lower next period our contractor would have been better off to wait before subcontracting. By the more complicated process of hedging, however, he can shift this risk, too. For example, a textile manufacturer expects to carry an inventory of cotton over into the next time period. If the price of cotton falls, he will lose money as compared to the alternative of not holding the inventory and buying cotton next period. If the price rises he will gain as compared to that alternative. Wishing to avoid the possibility of a loss, the manufacturer can do so, provided he is also willing to forgo the possibility of gain; that is, provided he simply wants to preserve the value of his inventory. The distinguishing feature of the cotton and some thirty other commodity markets in the United States is that you can buy and sell future as well as present goods on them. There is a market price for cotton to be delivered this period and another market price for cotton to be delivered in the next time period. Our manufacturer then becomes a futures seller: he agrees to deliver the amount of his inventory next period at the future price now being quoted on the market. Now if the price next period falls below the current-period futures price, his inventory is worth less, but he will make a compensating profit by buying at the now lower price and making his delivery of the cotton at the previously agreed higher price. The reverse happens if price next period rises above the current future price. Thus the manufacturer has succeeded in keeping the net value of his inventory at the current-period futures price level, regardless of future price changes.

Risk shifting generally makes it possible to simplify enterprise decision making. By taking out insurance the businessman avoids the necessity of constantly adjusting his financial position so as to be able to survive the relevant risks. The commodity hedger avoids the need to keep a close watch on the present and prospective price changes for one of his inputs. The forward sale contractor can now forget about price changes next period for some of the services he has agreed to supply. This releases information processing capacity of the enterprise to concentrate on other aspects of the business. Of course the decisions required to shift risk require some information to make wisely. But if the markets are well organized this is likely to be a relatively minor cost as compared to that of dealing directly with the risks.

Of course businessmen do not shift all risks on to others. Indeed they cannot. Where the risks themselves are relatively unknown they often can only be partially shifted, since the insurer will want to leave the risk shifter with an incentive to take ordinary precautions against unfavorable developments. And finally, in most businesses, an important source of profits is the opportunity the businessman has to use his ability and knowledge to exploit a limited range of risky situations to his own advantage. An obvious example of this is the collection of enterprises which were on the other end of the three types of risk-shifting deals described above. In each case a part at least of their business activity must have consisted in the absorption of the risks which were being shifted.

Note that every interperiod contract involves risk absorption by someone. In our forward-sales contract the subcontractor has assumed the risk of gain or loss if prices next period turn out to be higher or lower than that at which he made the deal. Of course he could hedge, too, by subcontracting himself, but eventually someone must absorb the risk of this change. In most markets a wide variety of alternative patterns of risk absorption may be observed. Provisions for reopening price negotiation if the market price changes significantly may be a part of the deal, thus leaving uncertain the question of who is to bear the risk.[1] Another common provision calls for some sharing of the risk among the parties.

A large firm which faces a great variety of risks may be in a position to insure itself, so to speak. When there are a lot of risks that are more or less independent of one another, many of the gains and losses will cancel each other out in each time period, so that increasing the size of a firm can be in itself a kind of risk shifting (with "nature" acting as the insurer!). The market recognizes this aspect of size by the willingness of lenders to provide credit to such firms at a somewhat lower price (interest rate) than to others.

It has already been noted that some economists doubt that the assumption of profit maximization is useful in analyzing enterprise behavior. In closing the present chapter we may note two technical difficulties in interpreting the concept of profit maximization, and suggest a connection between this problem and these doubts. The first has to do with the time dimension of profit maximization. We have been assuming that the businessman maximizes profits for each time period. But plainly this is not a good assumption when dealing with the outcomes with respect to two (or more) periods. For example, it would no doubt increase profits this period if the businessman arranged to just exhaust his inventories at the end of the period, for in this way he could keep the cost of storing goods down, at no cost to current revenue. But this could put him in serious trouble next period if it took any time to obtain new stocks, for his plant would have to be shut down in the meantime. So he must have next period in mind to some extent in making decisions this period. Indeed, all our decisions dealing with risk shifting were also decisions in which some current-period costs were being incurred in order to keep the risk of losses down next period.

This brings us to the second problem: what criterion should a businessman use in evaluating risk? At the moment we only point out that varying degrees of cautiousness are possible. Some may be less willing than others to run a given risk of ruin; they will be willing to pay a higher price for security, other things equal. Are they being less sensible?

These questions cannot be answered in a way that would be acceptable to all economists today. However, they point to the breadth of scope for interpreting the notion of profit maximization. When questions of the time horizon and the attitude toward risk of the decision maker are taken into account, many of the phenomena that are claimed to show the absence of profit maximization may

Profit Maximization—Is it True?

---

1. This action may be a useful way to avoid unnecessary negotiation. If prices do not change there is no reason to decide who bore the risk.

be reconciled with that notion. A firm that appears to be sacrificing current profits in order to capture a larger share of the market may be trying to maximize profits over a longer period of time, or may be running the risk of lower profits even in the longer run on the relatively small chance of a large increase in future profits. Profit maximization is a powerful if simple hypothesis and, properly interpreted, may even be useful in explaining quite complex phenomena.

7

Competition and Monopoly

One of the central aims of price theory is to provide information as to how efficient organization can be achieved in the production sector of the economy. The earlier discussion of markets argued that free exchange provides an efficient allocation of already produced goods, when each household or decision unit had on hand a stock of goods and was free to make or not make deals with other households for exchanges of those goods. Once all deals that were agreeable to the relevant pairs of decision units were made, it was not possible to increase the satisfaction of any household by a further deal that was acceptable to some other household. If all markets were in equilibrium, clearly this is the situation that would then hold in our market economy. In addition we saw that there are forces tending to push individual markets toward equilibrium.

In this chapter we want to take account of production and consider what effect alternative forms of productive organization have on efficiency. In particular we will study the reasoning behind the tendency for economists to prefer competition among a large number of units as the most efficient form of productive organization. Of course, like our propositions in this and previous chapters, the conclusions are a product of the assumptions, and the relevance of the conclusions to the real world depends on the realism of the key assumptions. Relevance also is dependent on the realism and power of alternative theories, since the economy is always with us and we must make decisions about it (even though the decision is to do nothing).

Our problem is to tie the analysis of the profit-maximizing firm of the last chapter to the analysis of markets. In dealing with the firm we took no account of its competitors. Ordinarily we think of the competitors as comprising an industry. But "industry" is a rather slippery term, partly because many individual firms produce a large number of different products, and partly because the products of different firms often vary in their properties (as with cigarettes and beer). But we faced this same problem in dealing with markets and can deal with it, at least for the moment, by definition. As in the case of markets we will be able to choose our scope of coverage for the industry to suit the particular problem with which we are concerned.

▶   *An industry is the collection of firms that make deals for the sale of products on a particular market.*

Monopoly   Now we may turn to the simplest form of industry and analyze the monopoly, in which there is only one firm selling the product. In fact we have already analyzed this case. The diagrams of Figure 6.3 fit the monopoly case very well. The firm faces a typical downward-sloping demand curve, with the marginal-revenue curve lying below. Costs are described in the marginal- and average-cost curves.

▶ ▶   *The monopoly maximizes its own (and consequently also industry) profits by producing at the output at which marginal cost equals marginal revenue. The price it charges is the price at which that output will be bought by consumers.*

Note that our monopolist really does not have a supply curve. Supply curves tell us how much will be offered on a market at any given price. But for the monopolist price is not given. The monopolist is able to take into account the different prices that he will be able to charge if he offers given different amounts on the market. Indeed this ability to set price is the source of his ability to generate extra profits.

Competitive   Now for the competitive firm. In our idealized picture of com-
Firm and   petition we assume that decision units are relatively very small.
Industry

▶   *A competitive industry is one in which firms are so small, relative to demand, that no one of them can have a significant effect on price by varying its own level of output.*

Such industries do exist. The wheat farmer faces a national market for his product and plainly has no individual control over price. Even in cotton production, where some enterprises are quite large, it is doubtful that any one producer could significantly affect the price of cotton by varying his own output on a free market. It may be that in some industries which have fewer than a hundred firms, none of whom are very large, competitive conditions are approximated.

What is the meaning of this assumption for the individual firm? Clearly its impact is on the firm's demand curve. A demand curve which shows that no variation in output will have any effect on price would be horizontal. In Figure 7.1 such a demand curve is drawn and the firm equilibrium shown.

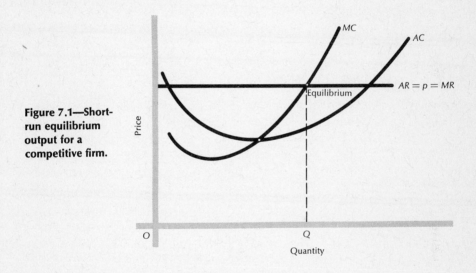

Figure 7.1—Short-run equilibrium output for a competitive firm.

► ► *For a horizontal demand curve, marginal revenue equals average revenue and, consequently, price.*

Average revenue is neither being pulled up nor down by marginal revenue, therefore it must be adding to total revenue exactly the amount of average revenue with each additional unit sold. On the cost side we see that

► ► *The competitive firm will supply to the market that level of output for which marginal cost equals price.*

Note that although marginal revenue equals average revenue, our earlier proposition that equilibrium occurs where marginal revenue equals marginal cost is not violated. We are dealing with a special case, resulting entirely from the horizontal demand curve.

►► *A competitive firm's supply curve coincides with the rising portion of its marginal-cost curve.*

Clearly this is true at the equilibrium point. The amount supplied at the equilibrium price is the amount determined by the intersection of the horizontal demand curve with the marginal-cost curve. Suppose now that the price is raised. The new equilibrium is then at a higher point on the same marginal-cost curve. Thus the marginal-cost curve does show the amount offered to the market by the firm at any given price.

This takes care of the competitive firm, but it does not yet tell us what happens on a market in which the firms are competitive. To do this we must put together or aggregate the results of the decisions of individual firms. This can be done for competitive firms just as it could for households in constructing demand curves. Each firm has its own supply curve, determined by the variation in individual marginal costs as output varies. For any given price we can find out from these curves how much each firm will supply to the market. The sum of these amounts gives us market supply. Given this information from individual firm supply curves we can calculate market supply for any given price, and so by varying price and making

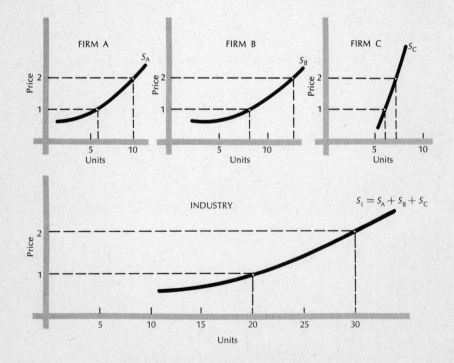

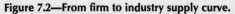

Figure 7.2—From firm to industry supply curve.

successive calculations can determine a market-supply curve. This is done in Figure 7.2 for a three-firm competitive industry.

▶ ▶ *In a competitive industry price and output are determined at the point where the aggregate marginal-cost curve intersects the industry-demand curve.*

We have already seen that the competitive firm's supply curve lies on its marginal-cost curve. This is true for the competitive industry as well. For each firm the marginal cost equals price, so marginal cost is the same for all firms at the assumed supply price. The quantity shown on the aggregate marginal-cost curve is, as noted above, the amount which all firms supply at that given price.

Now our analysis bears fruit in the sense that we can compare competitive and monopoly forms of organization.

Monopoly vs. Competition

▶ ▶ *A profit-maximizing monopoly will sell a smaller amount of goods at a higher price than a competitive industry faced with the same demand and cost situation.*

Figure 7.3 compares the competitive and monopoly situations. We may assume that the monopolist has the same number of plants as

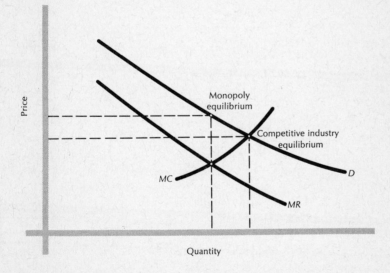

Figure 7.3—The monopolist produces less and gets a higher price.

the competitive industry, that costs are identical for both and that the industry absorbs only a small fraction of each input.[1] The monopolist has the same profit-maximizing incentive, so he will

1. The reason for this last assumption will become apparent in Chapter 8, pp. 104-105.

reduce costs wherever he can, just as the competitive firms do. Hence he will allocate a given amount of output among plants in exactly the same way as would occur under competition. If he did not, marginal costs would differ among plants and he could reduce total cost by producing a unit less in a high-marginal-cost plant and a unit more in a low-marginal-cost plant. For this reason the monopolistic and the competitive aggregate marginal-cost curves are identical. By assumption the demand curves facing both organizational forms are also identical. Clearly the shapes of cost and revenue curves we have assumed lead us to the above comparative proposition.

Now we come to the final step in this rather long chain of analysis:

► ► *If a monopolized industry were to become competitive, a more efficient allocation of national resources would result, provided all other industries were competitive.*

Suppose that in general industries are competitive, but that there is one monopolized industry. In the long run the competitive industries will be operating at the minimum point of their average-cost curves where average cost equals price. This is true because if the firms are making higher profits than are available in other industries there will be entry by new firms, driving prices down until no firm can enter successfully without another firm of comparable size leaving. At this point the profits earned are equal to the opportunity cost of investment elsewhere. Therefore, since all revenues can be allocated to opportunity costs, average cost equals price.

Given this situation, assume that a dollar's worth less output is produced in one of the competitive industries. This releases a dollar's worth of productive resources. Suppose these are allocated to the monopoly. If that industry had in fact been competitive, the dollar's worth of additional resources would have produced a dollar's worth of additional output because average cost would equal price. But since it is a monopoly the price that consumers are willing to pay is higher than the competitive price. Consumers are willing to pay more than a dollar for this additional output. That is, consumers would get more satisfaction from these resources if they were used in the monopoly than if they were used in one of the competitive industries. Therefore efficient production of consumer satisfaction would require that the industry produce more than the monopoly equilibrium output. This will continue to be true until that industry, too, is producing at the competitive level of output. At that point price will equal average cost and so a dollar's worth of additional inputs will produce only a dollar's worth of additional output.

In Chapter 4 we discussed the difficulties in measuring the total satisfaction generated in an economy and concluded that no generally accepted measure of total satisfaction existed. Nevertheless it is possible to come to some partial evaluation of different ways of organizing an economy by using a more limited approach to satisfaction measurement, one which parallels the concept of efficiency discussed in Chapter 5. Consider a set of alternatives for an economy which consists of different patterns of production and exchange of goods among decision units.

► *A given alternative is said to be Pareto optimal with respect to the others if it is not possible, by choosing one of the other alternatives instead of the given one, to increase the satisfaction of some decision units without reducing that of any of the others.*

The idea of Pareto optimality takes us a step beyond efficiency, since it makes comparisons in terms of the satisfaction obtained by individual households. Since it does not make comparisons between households, does not weigh my satisfaction against yours, it is free of any important kind of value judgment about which people are sure to differ. What Pareto optimality does do is identify alternatives which provide the most satisfaction, given that we do not make such value judgments. We are likely to be able to agree that the best alternative will be Pareto optimal with respect to others. Consequently if we can agree on the facts in a given situation and can identify the Pareto-optimal alternatives we have simplified the problem of choosing an alternative. From there on we must bring deeper value judgments to bear on the decision as to which of the remaining alternatives, all of which are Pareto optimal, is the best one.

Is competition Pareto optimal with respect to monopoly? That is, suppose we compare only two situations for an economy which satisfies the competitive assumptions about tastes and technology. In the first situation all firms are competitive. In the second one industry is monopolized and the remaining firms are competitive. Our question then is: Is the former situation Pareto optimal with respect to the latter? We can say this much right away: the answer is "no" unless the monopolist is no worse off under competition than he was under monopoly. This means clearly that, under the competitive alternative, he must be compensated in some way for his loss of control over the output of his former industry if that alternative is to be Pareto optimal.

Armed with this information we can now learn something more about our earlier assertion that a market economy is efficient. It now appears to be false, since market economies can contain monopolies. Actually the proposition is still true, but only because implicitly we were making a most unreasonable assumption about deals, namely that all deals that are mutually beneficial will be made. Thus we were assuming that all the participants in an economy who stand to gain from the shift from monopoly to competition—and there may be millions of them—offer a deal to buy out the monopolist and set up a competitive industry in his place. This ignores the tremendous information and negotiating costs that such a deal would inevitably entail. The problem here is that there is no market for the buying of monopolies and their conversion to competitive industries. As a reasonable assertion, the efficiency and freedom-maximizing property of markets applies, at best, only to the collection of potential and actual deals that markets do in fact mediate.

Without further ado let us take a big leap to the following proposition:

▶▶   *Under certain circumstances, competition produces results which are at least as good as those obtainable under any other type of economic organization.*

Up to this point we have tried to give at least some idea of the reasoning that lies behind our propositions. Unfortunately there is not space here to do the same thing for this last assertion. All that we can do is make a few comments on those "certain circumstances" that obviously loom large in the statement. Only a few of them will be listed below, but they are the most important ones.

1. When we say "at least as good as" what we really mean is that no other type of economic organization is Pareto optimal with respect to competition, unless competition is also Pareto optimal with respect to it. We are dealing with only a very limited kind of value judgment about the alternatives.

2. We have already mentioned the assumptions about the shapes of demand and cost functions. These must hold true, for if they do not, the equilibrium points may, for example, not be profit-maximizing points, or the markets may not be stable. Our hypothesized shapes are probably typical of real-world firms and markets but undoubtedly there are a number of exceptions. Some of the exceptions will come up later, as for example the case of the firm or industry whose average-cost curve declines to the right out to a point well beyond the output which would satisfy all reasonable demands for the good.

3. Technical independence is assumed for all decision units, households as well as firms. This means that no one decision unit can directly affect the satisfaction or production possibilities of other units by its behavior. For example, it assumes that my level of satisfaction depends only on the kinds and amounts of good I consume and not at all on your consumption. An example which applies to firms is that of apple growers and beekeepers. The amount of honey

that a beekeeper can harvest depends on the number of apple trees his neighbors grow, but the apple growers cannot keep the bees from taking nectar from apple blossoms, so the dependence is direct and not mediated by markets. Hence if beekeepers and apple growers operate separate contiguous farms our assumption is violated.

4.   There must be a good distribution of wealth in the society. In saying "good" we mean to make a value judgment. That is, even if all the other assumptions are satisfied, the competitive outcome is the best *for you* only if you believe that the distribution of wealth that exists in the society in question is just. This takes care of the situation—a perfectly possible one—in which competition produces, at equilibrium, starvation for those who have no valuable services to offer.

5.   All decision units are well informed. This means that households and firms know what goods are available, what their quality is, and at what prices they are being sold. It also means that households know what is best for themselves and that advertising does not confuse or mislead them.

6.   A final assumption to be mentioned is that, by and large, the entire collection of markets which constitute the economy is stable and that the economy tends to stay reasonably close to the equilibrium points in these markets. There is not much use in praising the equilibrium point toward which an economy tends if most of the time it is far away from that point.

Every one of these assertions raises all sorts of difficulties. In the American economy there are clearly exceptions to every assumption. Most of them are obvious. The existence of business fluctuations calls the last assumption into question. Clearly many households are very poorly informed about their alternatives and, even when they are informed, consumers seem to many of us not to know what is best for themselves. Many object to the way in which wealth is currently distributed, even with the substantial redistributions which the government is carrying out. Interdependence is claimed by many to be of the greatest importance for households and by no means unimportant in production. The question is: How much deviation is there and how destructive are these deviations for the theory? At the moment all we can say is that economists are by no means agreed on the answer, though they are agreed at least that the answer will vary to some extent, depending on the use to which the conclusion is to be put.

Finally, it might seem that our proposition offers a definitive answer to Socialists. If competitive capitalism cannot be improved on, why should anyone want to adopt socialism? There are several possible answers for a Socialist. One is that there are versions of socialism which can do as well as capitalism by simulating its procedures. Another possible answer is that socialism can do other things which capitalism cannot do as well, for example by providing an egalitarian distribution of wealth, which might not be feasible under a system of private ownership, where the owner has the right to free disposition of his own wealth (including the right to sell out to the wealthier). Another Socialist answer might be that independence of households is a bad thing. Socialists often talk about the collective spirit and solidarity; these ideas seem inconsistent with our notion of consumer independence. If they are successfully fostered by the Socialist state, a competitive outcome may be quite an inefficient one.

Thus the restrictions which our assumptions impose on the scope of our proposition also set limits to its relevance for settling some major policy issues of the time.

In Chapter 10 we will return to the evaluation of the usefulness of this proposition. It should be emphasized, however, that despite its limitations, this theory of efficient resource allocation plays a central role in many areas of economic analysis.

8

Factor Markets

In dealing with enterprise decision making in Chapters 6 and 7, we found that the profit-maximizing manager chose the level of output at which marginal revenue was equal to marginal cost. The marginal-revenue curve could be derived from demand conditions, which are given to the manager, a part of his environment. However, the origin of the cost curves was not given much attention. So in dealing with factor choice now we will be rounding out the theory of the firm by deriving cost from the market and technological data relating to factors of production. We will assume that there are diminishing marginal returns to each factor whose level of use is varied, and that the prices of each factor used by the enterprise are fixed by the market and known to the manager.

For any given level of output the manager will want to minimize his costs. If several alternative factor combinations are available, his choice will have a rather familiar property:

▶▶ *The least-cost factor combination is that one for which it is not possible to increase output by any reallocation from one factor to another of a dollar of expenditure.*

This sounds very much like the consumer's criterion for allocating

The Theory of Marginal Productivity

his budget expenditures. The only difference is in the "direction" of desired movement. The consumer was trying to get maximum satisfaction from a given dollar expenditure while the enterprise manager is trying (under present assumptions) to get a given output at minimum expenditure. Again the rule is almost self-explanatory. If you can get more output for a given expenditure, that is convincing evidence that you can get the same output for less.[1]

Given that this rule has been applied to the determination of the least-cost factor mix for each relevant level of output, it is easy to derive marginal cost. Marginal cost is simply the cost difference between the least-cost-factor mixes for two adjacent output levels. So we now have a two-stage theory of enterprise decision making:

▶ ▶ *The profit-maximizing manager first finds his least-cost-factor combinations and derives a marginal-cost curve from these; he then derives a marginal-revenue curve from his demand curve and finds the output at which marginal cost equals marginal revenue. This is his output choice.*

Armed with these rules for enterprise decision making when profit maximization is the goal we can now turn to the analysis of the forces of supply and demand on individual factor markets. In order to see the connections more clearly we will first restate the marginal-productivity rule.

▶ ▶ *The least-cost-factor combination can be found at that factor mix for which the ratio of marginal product[2] to factor price is the same for every factor used by the enterprise.*

Both forms of the rule require measurement of the productivity of one factor as compared to another. They differ only in the units employed. In the first rule it was the productivity of an additional *dollar's worth* of each factor; in the second it is the productivity of an additional *unit* of each factor. Hence in the second case marginal product comes in explicitly and the price of each factor must be brought in to provide a common dollar measure of the cost of an additional unit of each factor.

Since factors of production are bought and sold on markets we can analyze demand and supply influences on one of them separately, just as we would for a product market. We will start with the demand side and assume at the beginning that factor prices are

1. For example take the new, higher-output combination and reduce each factor use proportionately until the desired output level is reached. Note that the only hindrance to this approach is lumpiness of factors or of production processes. In that case the rule is only an approximation to the minimum cost combination.
2. See chapter 5, page 63 for definition.

given to the enterprise. We will also consider only a single-factor market, assuming that all other factors are in fixed supply to the enterprise. The technological alternatives open to the enterprise are shown on Figure 8.1, where the marginal product associated with

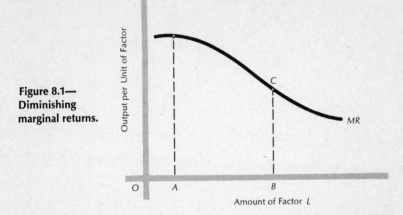

**Figure 8.1—
Diminishing
marginal returns.**

increasing use of the variable factor L are depicted. Notice that diminishing marginal returns set in if more than OA of factor L is used, given the existing levels of use of the other factors. Notice also the peculiar nature of demand on a factor market:

► ►   *The demand for a factor of production is a derived demand;
that is, it stems not from the value of the factor itself as a
final good but from its usefulness in producing final goods.*

There is easy-to-hand a measure of the usefulness of a factor, at least to the enterprise. This is the marginal revenue of an additional unit of output. At any given level of factor use, such as OB in Figure 8.1, there is a marginal product, in this case BC, which measures the additional output obtained from a unit increase in the use of Factor L when OB of the factor is already being used. The marginal revenue tells us how much additional revenue each of those additional units of output will bring in.[3] Thus the usefulness of the additional unit of the factor is measured by the product of these two—marginal revenue times marginal product.

On Figure 8.2 the curve MRP shows the usefulness of an additional unit of factor L at various levels of use of L. It is derived from the MP (marginal product) curve of Figure 8.1 by simply multiplying each marginal product by the appropriate marginal revenue, which in turn is derived from the demand curve at the relevant level of product output.

3. Assuming that the marginal product is small enough that there is not a significant change in price as a result of such a small increase in deliveries to the product market.

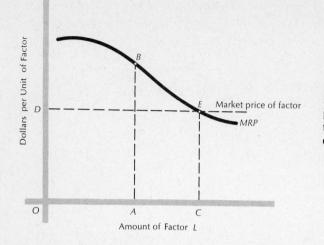

Figure 8.2—
Marginal-revenue
product and
factor-market
equilibrium.

▶ *The marginal revenue product is the increase in revenue to a firm from (1) a small increase in the use of a factor and (2) the sale at market price of the resulting increase in output.*

The curve is called the marginal-revenue product curve since it measures marginal-revenue products, such as *AB*, associated with given levels of factor use—in this case, *OA*.

Thus the marginal-revenue product measures the usefulness of a given small additional use of a factor. The cost of the addition is easy to measure: it is simply the price of the factor. This leads us to the market adjustment rule for the case where price is given.

▶▶ *The enterprise will continue to add units of a factor of production so long as the marginal-revenue product exceeds the given factor price. Equilibrium use of the factor occurs at the point where marginal-revenue product equals factor price.*

In Figure 8.2 factor use *OA* is clearly nonoptimal. At that point an additional unit of the factor adds *AB* dollars to revenue and only *OD* dollars to cost, so adding a unit of the factor will increase profits. Beyond *OC* the reverse is true. Hence profits are maximized at *OC* where marginal-revenue product *CE* is exactly equal to factor price *OD*.

Marginal-productivity theory puts great emphasis on the close connection between the price a factor receives and the market value of the product it produces. There have been many criticisms of the theory, both on the grounds of empirical relevance and because of its apparent implication that in a competitive economy the factors of production "earn what they get." In the following sections the analysis of particular types of factor markets will shed some further light on the significance of the theory in the light of these criticisms.

There are three ways in which these results can be generalized to give a much more powerful theory of the determination of factor-market demand. The first involves relaxing the assumption that all other factors are in fixed supply to the enterprise. The above equilibrium condition applies to each factor market for which factor use can vary. Notice that all three of our rules for factor choice now become equivalent. The last of these says:

Marginal revenue times marginal product equals factor price (now extended to apply to each factor market). Rearranging terms, this becomes

$$\frac{1}{mr} = \frac{mp}{p_f}.$$

But the marginal revenue in equilibrium must be the same with respect to each factor market, since the same level of output determines marginal revenue in each case. So our rule says the ratio of marginal product to price must be the same for each factor, which is precisely the second version of the marginal-productivity rule. Our third rule includes the previous rule as a special case and adds a new condition —on marginal-revenue product—to select that particular least-cost-factor mix which also maximizes profit.[4]

The second extension is from enterprise to market. All firms making use of a given factor have a derived demand for that factor. The total market demand for the factor will be the sums of the demands of individual units at various factor prices. Typically the demanders will produce a variety of products which are in turn sold on markets with a variety of structures; some may be monopolies, others competitive. But this is all taken account of by the marginal-productivity rule which is stated in terms of marginal revenue. And it measures usefulness to the enterprise in comparable dollar terms rather than in the disparate units of the products themselves. The principle of diminishing marginal returns gives a strong presumption that derived demand curves will be downward sloping.

►► *Thus the aggregated marginal-revenue product curves combined with marginal-productivity theory gives us a set of market-demand curves for factors of production with the ordinary properties.*

4. A difficulty may have occurred to some readers. When adjustment leads to an increase in the use of one factor, this in turn may increase the productivity of the others, thereby shifting their marginal product curves up. These shifts may indeed occur but they do not affect the validity of the marginal productivity rule. The equilibrium still must have the stated property if profit is to be maximized.

Finally we may relax the assumption that the price of the factor is given. It is not uncommon to find that increasing use of a factor will lead to an increase in the price required to obtain an additional unit of the factor, especially in the short run. This case of rising supply curves is depicted in Figure 8.3. If firms demanding the factor are numerous and small they will not be able to take any monopolistic

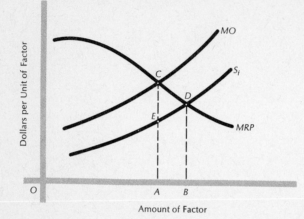

Figure 8.3—The buyer with monopoly power buys less and pays less than under competition when the supply curve is rising.

advantage of rising supply, finding that their own use of the factor is an insignificant fraction of total demand. Taking price as fixed the market would produce an equilibrium at factor use *OB* with the price of the factor being fixed at *BD*.

Suppose, however, that there is only one firm which uses this particular factor. The supply curve S_f implies that there are many small suppliers of this factor to the market. The monopolist[5] can now take advantage, in a familiar way, of the fact that varying his use of the factor will vary its price significantly. He now derives the factor-market opposite number to the marginal-revenue curve. This curve, called the marginal-outlay curve, lies above the rising supply curve for exactly the same reason that the marginal-revenue curve lies below the falling demand curve. In each case the monopolist has an opportunity to make more profits by taking advantage of his ability to influence price. In the present case he knows that if he hires an additional amount of the factor he will have to pay more two ways: first he has to pay more to the additional factor than he did to previous units, and second he must pay more to the intramarginal factor units. This is because a new and higher market equilibrium price for the factor has been set as a result of his increased demand. Thus the total additional cost to him of buying an additional amount of the

5. Because he is now the sole buyer rather than, as in Chapter 7, the sole seller, he is sometimes called a *monopsonist.*

factor is greater than the factor price. The marginal-outlay curve shows total additional factor cost at each level of factor use. For example, at *OA* level of factor use in Figure 8.3 an additional unit of the factor will cost *EA*. But because of the rising supply price the total additional cost will be *CA*. This just equals marginal-revenue product, so *OA* is the equilibrium factor use level and *EA* the price paid for each unit of the factor by our businessman.

▶ ▶   *In a competitive factor market the factor price is set by the intersection of factor supply with the aggregated marginal-revenue product curves of factor users. If the demand side of the market is monopolized, and the supply curve is rising, both factor price and factor use will be lower than in the competitive case.*

The Aggregate Supply Curve for Labor

Let us begin by thinking in very general terms. Forgetting about differences among laborers and kinds of labor we treat the supply and demand for labor as a single market, the collection of all deals involving the buying and selling of labor services. A kind of average wage will be our notion of the price of labor. There will be in this case the usual marginal-revenue product curve determining demand for labor, and clearly in the United States economy this will not be a monopoly demand. Since only a quarter of the American labor force is unionized, the supply side, too, is not monopolized. On the supply side laborers have only a twofold choice: either to work at the going wage or to be at leisure but without pay. The interaction of choices on both sides of the market determines the equilibrium aggregate price of labor.

What will the supply curve for labor look like? Considering the kind of averaging that must be done to obtain such a supply curve, it is understandable that we do not have too clear a picture of its actual shape. But at least we can discuss a few of its properties.

In the first place, except for the very rich (and the very lazy), at least one member of each family will be eager to work; that is, such people will tend to place a rather low value on leisure. In some countries—India for example—a wage of a dollar a day will suffice to bring most such people (remember: on the average!) into the labor market willing to work. In the United States this is not true. Even a dollar an hour probably would not attract a large fraction of the potential breadwinners. One important reason for this is custom. We have become accustomed to a very much higher standard of living than have the Indians. Consequently our conception of what constitutes a subsistence or living wage tends to be very different from

Labor Markets

an Indian's. Of course this may not be an immutable state of affairs. If a nuclear war destroyed our productive facilities, the acceptable wage for surviving breadwinners might decline very sharply and quickly. And with economic development Indian standards will doubtless rise.

Another reason for the high minimum acceptable wage is government policy. The governments of the United States, like those of other countries, have assumed some measure of responsibility for seeing that people do not starve. Also for most lines of work the Federal government has set minimum wage levels, making it illegal to pay less. Consequently the leisure choice in the United States typically does not imply an absolute zero level of income, and, in addition, the supply curve is not allowed to fall below the minimum wage.[6]

It seems likely that, over the lower reaches of the supply curve, as the price of labor rises, so will the amount of labor offered to the market. Partly this is due to the increasing number of breadwinners— of first members of the family to work—entering the market. Partly it is due to the gradual entry of second and third members of the family. As housewives and teenagers begin to see opportunities to increase the family income and their own individual income as the wage rises, "leisure" becomes relatively less attractive. But there is also a tendency acting in the opposite direction. On the one hand the higher wage makes an additional unit of paid work a better substitute for nonwork. On the other hand, the higher income may make the additional satisfaction of another dollar of income relatively less attractive than the previous dollars. This will be true if the marginal utility of income is decreasing. A point may be reached beyond which the latter effect becomes dominant. In this case further increases in the price of labor may lead some to drop out of the labor market. The supply curve of labor then begins to bend backward toward the vertical axis, as is shown far out on the supply curve of Figure 8.4. Some economists believe that we have occasionally reached this section of the supply curve.

Another point concerns shifts in the supply curve. We have already mentioned one instance of this—the shift in attitudes toward subsistence that a sudden and drastic change in the economic environment might induce. This implied a downward shift in the supply curve, so that at any given price more labor will be offered, provided we are within the upward-sloping portion of the curve. Another shift has probably been occurring in recent years. Attitudes toward working women have been undergoing a long-term shift in the

6. Since not all types of labor are covered, this statement is not precisely true. But it serves well enough for our aggregative assessment of supply factors.

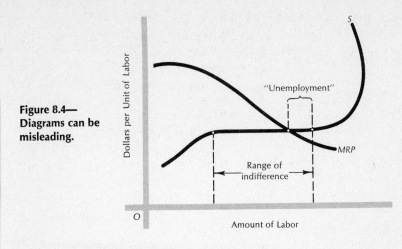

Figure 8.4—Diagrams can be misleading.

United States so that under comparable conditions more women are probably willing to work at a given level of male employment today than was the case forty years ago. At the same time, however, increasing affluence has probably changed attitudes toward appropriate wages somewhat, which would tend to shift the aggregate supply curve up. These and other trend factors make it very difficult to isolate the supply curve empirically.

A final point concerns the difficulty in interpreting the idea of aggregate unemployment. If the labor market is in equilibrium and the supply curve of labor is rising, then there is no unemployment in the sense that everyone who is willing to work at the market price of labor, or less, is employed. Unemployment could occur if the supply curve were perfectly horizontal, for then more people may offer themselves at the going rate than are demanded. But this kind of unemployment is trivial. Perfectly elastic or horizontal supply means, in a market containing freely choosing, independent individuals, that people are virtually indifferent to working or not working at the going price. This is true because, though they are willing to work at the going rate, if that rate were reduced just a little they would drop out of the market. This situation is described diagrammatically in Figure 8.4. Such unemployment can hardly be viewed as a serious social problem.

Have we succeeded in proving that in a market economy unemployment is a figment of the imagination? Hardly. Instead we have illustrated some of the difficulties with this form of partial equilibrium analysis. Our model of the economic world has failed to provide useful results in this particular case. There are several reasons, but probably the most important one is the implicit assumption that demand and supply curves are independent. In dealing with such a large col-

Aggregate Unemployment

lection of deals as the labor market we have been neglecting the interconnections of economic processes. If, from a position of equilibrium, the marginal-revenue product curve for labor were to shift downward, this leads to workers being laid off. When the incomes of these workers fall they spend less and this, acting through derived demand, shifts the marginal-revenue product curve still further down. The assumption of relative independence of the two curves, which often works well when dealing with relatively small segments of the economy, breaks down when we try to analyze a large portion of the economy.

Another mistake lies not so much in the supply and demand curves themselves as in our interpretation of them. In fact a considerable part of the unemployment that occurs in market economies may be well described by the horizontal supply curve of Figure 8.4. The problem is that it is not the indifference of laborers to whether they work or not but institutional obstacles to reducing the wage rate that make supply appear to be horizontal. If employers fear that existing workers will strike or otherwise lower their productivity, or that the government will interfere in their decisions, or that a general reduction in wages will lose them their most productive workers, they may be reluctant to impose the lower wage. In this case the horizontal portion of the supply curve depicts an administered price—one which, at least in the short run, market forces cannot budge. What is at fault this time is our interpretation of labor supply as consisting of independent, freely choosing individuals.

A final simplifying assumption which turns out to be misleading in this case is the result of averaging all kinds of labor and wages together into a simple, single supply curve. This leaves out of account in our analysis the important so-called frictional unemployment. Frictional unemployment results when falling demand or technical changes lead to layoffs in some branches of the economy. It may take quite awhile for the laid-off workers to find new jobs even when the demand for labor is high. In a growing economy one or two per cent of the labor force may be in this position: it, too, is a casualty of our too simple picture of economic interaction. These difficulties with supply-demand analysis point the moral that care must be chosen in using simplified descriptions. Often they are very helpful, but this is true only if the right simplifications have been chosen for the problem at hand! The idea of an aggregate supply and demand curve for labor is useful in discussing in general terms the longer-run determinants of supply and demand, as we did earlier, but can be misleading in discussing the problems of unemployment in market economies.

Our partial equilibrium framework can, however, be useful in explaining another important aspect of the position of labor in a market
economy. There are very great wage differences among occupations
and among individuals in the United States, as in most other economies. What is the explanation of these differences? Three influences
on wage differentials are illustrated in the three panels of Figure 8.5.

**Labor Mar-
kets: Wage
Differentials
and Distri-
bution**

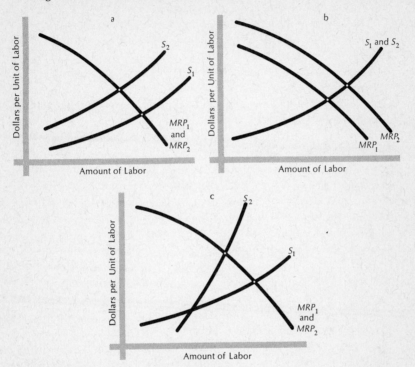

**Figure 8.5—Nature of the work, requirements of the work, and monopoly
power as influences on wage differentials.**

Turning first to Figure 8.5a, suppose that two industries have identical labor-demand curves. However, work in industry 2 is hard and
unpleasant while working conditions in industry 1 are relatively attractive. The consequence is that, other things being equal, more
people will be willing to work in industry 1 than in industry 2 at a
given wage. The supply curve for industry 2 therefore lies above that
of industry 1 and equilibrium will occur at a higher wage and lower
level of employment in the former industry. Because in this case the
higher wage compensates for less attractive working conditions, differentials of this kind are called *equalizing differences* in wages.

Now consider Figure 8.5b. In this case working conditions and skill
levels are comparable in two industries so that the supply curves are

identical. However, workers in industry 2 have a much higher marginal-revenue product than those in industry 1 at comparable levels of employment. This is because more of other factors, probably especially capital, is applied per worker in industry 2. As a result a different equilibrium is reached in industry 2 with higher wages paid and more workers employed.

In case (b) the question arises as to how the two separate supply curves can exist if the work uses comparable skill levels and involves comparably attractive working conditions. Would it not be more reasonable to aggregate both supply and both demand curves and treat them as a single market for the combined type of labor? In that case the wage would be the same in both industries. But if the kind of skill required takes some time and effort to acquire, there will not in fact be free movement from one industry to another in the short run. For example, though the skill levels are comparable, the typical machinist is not qualified as an electrician. What we would expect is that over the longer run the wage rates would equalize as new workers chose to learn the skill appropriate to the higher paid industry, and perhaps as some workers from industry 1 learned the skills appropriate to industry 2. But in the short run these differences in productivity of labor may create differences in wages.

A third kind of wage difference is illustrated in panel (c). In both industries there are comparable levels of productivity of labor and comparable working conditions. The different supply curves are a result of imperfections on the supply side of the market. A guild or union controls entry into the labor force of industry 2, thereby restricting supply and gaining a higher wage for the fortunate few. The same result might occur if the labor market fails to provide the necessary information about job alternatives. People of a particular social or ethnic background, or those in small towns and on farms are not aware of, or are socially excluded from the opportunities in industry 2, so that the offer of labor to this industry is kept below that of industry 1. The differential that exists in the United States between Negro and white wages might be partly explained on these grounds. This case is often called that of wage differences due to existence of noncompeting groups.

No one worker in the United States has much knowledge about job opportunities or about opportunities open to him to increase his skill levels, or in general to increase his attractiveness as a higher-paid worker. This suggests that the labor market may operate very imperfectly, with jobs often going begging because of ignorance or lack of foresight on both sides of the market. However, there is an aspect of the way markets work which probably leads the casual observer to understate the effectiveness of markets in allocating labor. This is the familiar idea of adjustment at the margin. Most workers are reasonably content in their present jobs and reasonably secure. For them to take the time and effort to study alternative employment opportunities carefully would be a malallocation of their time and energy. Instead, at any point in time only a small fraction of the labor force is dissatisfied and looking around. They, too, probably do not search very effectively. In most countries the government steps in to help organize this search process by creating employment offices in major employment areas. Also private employment agencies exist to help organize, for a price, information about market opportunities. But not even all the dissatisfied workers need know all the alternatives. If each covers an overlapping range of alternatives in his search, the market can perform its allocative function fairly effectively and at a great saving of time and effort to all.

The question of income distribution is discussed in the final chapter of this book. As for the effects on income distribution of a market economy, there are two that should be borne carefully in mind. The first is that

▶ ▶ *If markets are competitive and there is an appropriate amount of knowledge of alternatives and the right kind of production technology, then paying wages in accord with marginal productivity means efficiency in resource allocation.*

That is, it would not be possible to produce more of any one good without having to make do with less of some other good; and it would not be possible to produce that output with less of any one factor without increasing the use of some other factor.

The second point is that an efficient economy may nevertheless have a very bad distribution of income; for example, it conceivably might lead to a situation in which a few were very rich and the rest were starving.

The distinguishing feature of capital goods is that it is not reasonable to assume that the economic services they render and the cost of producing them all occur during a single time period. One can obtain the services of a laborer for a week or a month or a year and pay him during the period in which he renders his services. Not so for a factory, which may have taken a year to produce, and which may last for twenty years. So the special problem posed by capital is to find a means of comparing costs and revenues which are incurred in different time periods.

Capital and Time

The interest rate is a device by which these values can be compared. Let us suppose that a businessman is choosing between two alternative ways to produce the same output. In both cases the output will only be available in the next time period and the businessman is already committed to provide the goods then. One way of producing the good, the labor-intensive (or more or less handmade) way, means postponing production until the next period, since the good is delivered in the same period in which it is produced. (See Table 8.1.)

Table 8.1—Cost of Production for Two Projects Yielding Identical Outputs

Cost in Period:	Project	
	No. 1	No. 2
No. 1	0	100
No. 2	108	0

Cost of production in this case is $108. The other way, which is capital-intensive, requires that the factory be built in the current period, which will then be capable of supplying the goods next period. It costs $100 this period to produce the factory and accumulate the goods, and will cost nothing next period to supply the goods. However, after next period the factory will be worthless. So our businessman's decision is simply a matter of whether to pay $100 this period or $108 next period.

The market interest rate can be used to solve this problem for the businessman. It tells him the cost of borrowing or lending. If the interest rate is 4 per cent per period, he can borrow $100 this period provided he is willing to pay $104 next period. As a profit maximizer he is interested in producing the goods at minimum cost. Suppose he has $100 on hand. If he chooses the second project he simply spends this money on the capital goods. If he chooses the first project, however, he will not let his money remain idle during this period but will lend it out at interest. At a 4 per cent interest rate he will have $104 at the start of next period. But this is not enough to complete project 1; hence project 1 does not minimize his cost. Had the interest rate been above 8 per cent, project 1 could have been built while leaving a little extra cash; it would then have been preferable to project 2, which leaves him with no spare cash. So using the interest rate to compare costs in different time periods showed the businessman how costs could be minimized. Exactly the same approach makes possible the comparison of revenues earned in different time periods.

The market interest rate is established on the capital market, where capital goods are bought and sold. However, the buying and selling of capital goods is only part of the function of the capital market. In order to get a glimpse into its functioning, let us first consider why an individual might prefer to have a good in one period rather than another—or, to put it another way, why he might be willing to pay a premium in order to have the good in a particular period.

There are several reasons why an individual might prefer the present to a future period. One important consideration is that the future is less certain. He is not absolutely sure he has a future or, even if he does, whether the goods he wants will be available or will be particularly attractive to him. Secondly he may, especially if he is fairly young, expect to improve his economic position in the future. If his marginal utility of income is declining then he will prefer not to forgo a present consumption which produces more satisfaction. Thirdly he may expect the economy to grow. Even if his own relative position in society does not change, if more goods are available, standards of living in general will be higher and, again, the declining marginal utility of income will lead him to prefer present consumption.

Notice that none of these reasons apply to everyone; in each case there will probably be some who feel exactly the opposite about consumption. A soldier may defer consumption gladly till a time when he is in a better position to indulge his tastes; a family may have declining income (or children soon to go to college); and the output of an economy occasionally declines. And notice also that none of the reasons is absolute. That is, a family that prefers present consumption may nevertheless defer consumption and lend a portion of its income (for example, by putting it in a time deposit in a bank) if the interest rate is high enough. Thus the interest rate serves as a kind of balancing mechanism for the various present-future tastes of households and businesses.

Many of the people who appear as deal makers on the capital market (our saver of the preceding paragraph is of course one of these, and so are borrowers) are thus not buying or selling capital goods in the sense of factors of production, but rather are adjusting their time patterns of consumption in order to obtain the most satisfaction from them. So we have two functions for the capital market: (1) it serves to place comparable values on capital goods so that alternative factor mixes can be chosen which will maximize profits; (2) it serves to make possible adjustments of household-consumption patterns over time in an efficient way. There is yet a third way in which the capital market directly influences the economy: (3) it helps determine the portion of output that is assigned to increasing the capital stock. By comparing both revenues and costs over time, businessmen can estimate the profitability of alternative projects. The market interest rate tells them which projects are more profitable uses of their money than lending the money to others would be. The higher the interest rate, other things being equal, the fewer the profitable investment projects.

One final point about the interest rate. In practice there are a great many interest rates. This is not necessarily because the capital market is in disequilibrium. In fact many capital markets are so well organized that adjustment to equilibrium occurs in minutes instead of days. Rather it is a sign that there are a number of different goods being traded on the market, or to put it another way, there are many capital markets. A major dimension on which loans and capital goods differ is risk. Simply because the future is so deeply entwined in these goods there is bound to be a large and variable element of uncertainty as to whether the estimated profitability of a venture is likely to occur in practice. For example, loans to consumers for the purchase of automobiles generally carry some three times the interest rate as do short-term loans to large corporations. The potential dealer on capital markets can satisfy his tastes for risk and for a time pattern of consumption different from that of his income at one and the same time.

Rent   Rent is another of those terms that economists use in a different sense than does the rest of the citizenry.

▶   *Economic rent is the return to a factor beyond that necessary to keep it in its present use over some time period.*

The classic case of economic rent is that of land, and it may still serve to bring out the key aspect of rent. In Figure 8.6a the amount

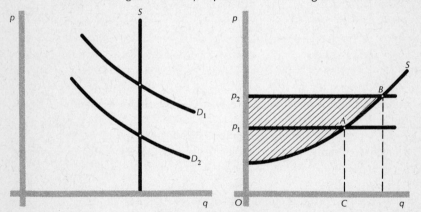

Figure 8.6—Economic rent.

of land available is fixed over the relevant time period. Any positive price will be preferred by the owners to no return at all. Hence, by definition, all their income from the land is rent. The opportunity cost of not using the land is zero. As shown in the diagram, a downward shift in demand has no effect on the amount supplied to the market.

Notice that ordinary rent often is not economic rent. For example, a new home can be built in a few weeks or months, so that varying price can effect the amount supplied over time periods of such length.

However, in most cases economic rent is combined with other types of factor income. Figure 8.6b illustrates this situation for a factor of production. From an initial equilibrium A at price p_1, a demand shift leads to a new equilibrium at the higher price p_2. But OC of the factor was available to the market at the old price of p_1. Hence all the increase in returns to these units of the factor constitutes rent. Altogether the entire shaded area measures the economic rent paid out to this factor at an equilibrium price of p_2. Price equals opportunity cost only for the last unit hired when the supply curve is rising to the right.

The fact that rent can be diverted from the resource owner without affecting the supply of the resource suggests rent as a leading candidate for taxation. The tax would not interfere directly with efficient resource allocation. Some have argued that because supply is not affected the owner of such a resource has no right to the returns which, as Figure 8.6 shows, the market will provide him. This aspect of the argument we will postpone until the final chapter. However, two points may be made now with respect to the effects of diverting rents from fixed-supply resource owners.

The first point is that though the act of diverting the returns does not affect resource allocation, the spending of the funds by some other agent certainly does have an effect. A different pattern of demand for resources results (unless the new holders of the funds spend them in exactly the same way as would the old). Consequently the assessment of the desirability of economic rent as a tax must take into account the other consequences of the act of diversion. This means either comparing the two patterns of demand or comparing the rent tax with alternative kinds of taxes.

The second point is that economic rent is difficult to estimate in practice. Partly this is because a resource rarely earns only rent. Since rent is in effect the amount paid a factor beyond its opportunity cost —that is, beyond its value in its next best use—rent is "pure" only when the opportunity cost is zero. But land, for example, is generally improved or altered in some way by human action and the kinds of alterations that can be or have been performed on it are many and are not separated by the market from one another, except in a very crude way. Partly the difficulty stems from the fact that to a limited extent supply of even the most fixed asset may vary. This is because holders of the asset may bargain with buyers, for supply is an economic, not a technological concept. The apartment owner does not accept the early offers for his apartments because he believes the equilibrium rent is higher. Until the equilibrium is established and generally recognized the supply available at a given price may be quite variable. Uncertainty about equilibrium, and the incentive to take advantage of uncertainty on the other side of the market make it worthwhile for the owner of the asset to hold it off the market even though there is no alternative valuable use for the asset. Another way of saying this is that it often is not clear to the outsider just what the opportunity cost of a particular factor is.

These are some of the reasons why economic rent has proved to be a rather difficult factor return to isolate in practice.

Entrepeneur- Our discussion to this point has failed to take proper account of
ship the organizational complexities of modern enterprise. A going concern is faced with a large-scale job of collecting and analyzing information as a preliminary to decision making. The decisions themselves require deliberation and a high level of skill. Possibly the future life, and certainly the future profits of the enterprise depend on these decisions. Even more delicate in the balancing of more or less imponderable factors is the decision to start a new enterprise, or to develop and market a new product. Entrepreneurship is the name given to the special skill required to make these decisions wisely.

We have seen that, at least in principle and ignoring risk, it is possible, using marginal-productivity theory, to isolate the earnings of individual factors of production and, at least under competitive conditions to relate these earnings to the productivity of the factor. It would certainly be useful to have such a measure for the key factor of entrepreneurship. A number of attempts have been made to isolate entrepreneurship but the task, even in principle, seems rather hopeless.

Two examples of rather extreme cases will illustrate one aspect of the problem. An existing enterprise has sold some bonds to the public. Since these constitute debt and the enterprise has been earning enough to pay the interest obligations to its creditors, these bondholders have no influence on enterprise decision making. The stockholders, however, are few in number and have most of their resources tied up in the company. Consequently they are extremely interested in all basic decisions relating to the enterprise. They in effect constitute the board of directors. They have chosen a manager with care and limit his discretion to day-to-day implementation of the instructions they pass on to him. In this case neither bondholders nor manager have any significant entrepreneurial function. The latter is a worker and the former are debt holders, no more. The stockholders themselves perform the entrepreneurial function.

Now consider a second firm. In this case there are a large number of stockholders, none of whom holds more than a very few per cent of the voting stock outstanding; nor do any of them have a substantial fraction of their own resources tied up in stock in this company. Stockholders in this case are interested in getting a reasonable dividend and a modicum of capital gains through increases in the value of their stock each year. So long as the company performs comparatively well by this measure, the stockholders have little interest in the precise nature of the decisions taken within the firm. The manager is thus in a position to do pretty much as he will. He may even be able to appoint members of the board of directors so that, unless he fails very badly, he is largely his own boss. Under these circumstances the stockholders of the company are not much different in their function than were the bondholders of the previous case, while the entrepreneurial function has been shifted to the manager.

Examples of this kind are not without their real-world counterparts. Also there are a variety of intermediate situations. It is even possible for bondholders to assume entrepreneurial functions. One way it can happen is if a company is forced into receivership. Then debt holders may have a voice in determining future policy, at least until the company is able to re-establish its creditworthiness. Another way in which it can happen, this time to a going concern, is if an enterprise makes frequent use of debt to finance its operations. By having a representative of the debtors on its board, participating in decision making, it may establish a more favorable market for its debt instruments. Presumably this fact will be reflected in the returns to some of the debt holders. These examples suggest that the market does not provide a simple measure of the returns to entrepreneurship, since these are paid out now in the form of profits to stockholders—now in the form of wages and bonuses to top management, now in the form of payments to bondholders.

The fact that entrepreneurship cannot be isolated easily as a factor share does not mean that the function is unimportant. Quite the contrary; it is certainly an essential ingredient of a dynamic economy. What it does imply is that converting a good idea successfully into useful goods and services is typically a complex process in which a number of people participate and, in a sense, share the "returns to entrepreneurship." An investor who agrees to help finance the new idea, even though he is merely buying bonds of the new company, is participating in this function. No doubt the venture is riskier than many others and this fact will be reflected in the interest rate offered with the bonds. To a limited extent some of the workers of such an enterprise are sharing in the function. The inconvenience of moving to a new location or of risking loss of seniority elsewhere or of risking a layoff during the next recession if the idea fails, suggests this involvement. It should be remembered that a mere look at the price of the bond or the wage rate does not convey enough information for the participants to make a wise decision. They do not know if the offered price is an equilibrium price, which might be compared with other market-equilibrium prices to evaluate potential returns and costs of buying in. Only by a fairly careful study of the economic potential of the idea can they provide a basis for wise decision making. And the more important the decision, other things being equal, the more time and effort that can be expended rationally in collecting and analyzing information beyond the price of the offered commodity. In all these cases some of this time and effort expended serves the entrepreneurial function.

In dealing with rent, capital, and entrepreneurship we have noted the difficulty in disentangling these functional shares from one another. It is important not to exaggerate the implications of this difficulty. There are strong cases in which the functional responsibility, and even the factor earnings, can be isolated to a useful degree of accuracy. And the difficulty points clearly to the fact that the market mechanism is a complex human organization, not a simple mechanical machine. The market system serves to organize and greatly simplify the information needed to make appropriate decisions. But it does not hand the right decisions to participants on a silver platter.

9

Bargaining

So far we have taken a look at only two kinds of market structure, competition and monopoly. According to our models, one of these is "good" and the other "bad" in the sense that one is consistent with an efficient allocation of economic resources while the other produces inefficiency from the point of view of providing consumers with maximum satisfaction. However, in the United States monopoly is illegal in most industries, and where it does exist its price and output and investment policies are generally regulated by the government. If we take competitive market structure to imply that no firm in the industry can have a significant effect on price by varying its own output then it too is relatively rare in the United States and elsewhere. Most industries seem to lie somewhere in between these two extremes. Therefore one of the more important questions from the point of view of evaluating the efficiency of a functioning market economy is whether these in-between types of industries come closer to the monopoly form or the competitive ideal in their behavior.

A notable feature of many of the intermediate industry structures is that bargaining plays an important role in the behavior of participants.

▶ *Economic bargaining is the discussion of the properties of deals that might be made by the participants.*

Usually bargaining contains a special feature: the simulation of preferences by the participants. Each side attempts to convey a somewhat misleading impression of its aims with a view to improving the benefits assigned to that side by the final deal.

Bargaining is ubiquitous in a market economy. In one form or another it occurs among members of the same industry, between large organizations facing one another across the market, such as union and management or government and industry, and is a part of the process of making a large fraction of the deals that are made (and those that are not as well) on most markets. It is even to be found on some markets that pass the above test of competitiveness. In the present chapter we survey some of the implications of bargaining for the allocation of resources and the price system.

Oligopoly: Why It Occurs

Oligopoly is the situation in which only a few firms dominate the industry. It is very common in manufacturing industries in the United States and in other developed market economies. Several of the reasons for its widespread occurrence require some comment.

Some technologies do not permit competition to survive.

▶▶ *A competitive market structure cannot persist in the long run where there are decreasing average costs over the range of demand.*

Suppose the industry consisted originally of a large number of small firms. The difficulty is illustrated in Figure 9.1. Since average cost is declining up to the point at which it crosses the demand curve, the marginal-cost curve lies below average cost over this range. The enterprises in this industry will individually expand the scale of their operations to try to take advantage of the lower costs at higher output levels. Those who do not expand fast enough will drop out because the competition of the larger firms is continually forcing price down. But even after there are only a few survivors, if competitive practices continue, all may go out of business. This can be seen from the fact that marginal cost crosses the demand curve at E where price, EF, is smaller than average cost, GF. At that price, the efficient competitive price, total cost exceeds total revenue. Of course long before this happened the larger firms would recognize their influence over price. If there was only one survivor and he was able to maximize profits without fear of government intervention he could earn the nice profits represented by the box $JKCD$ in Figure 9.1. Though we have drawn in only the industry curve, such a situation might permit several firms to operate profitably while selling at a price substantially above the competitive price.

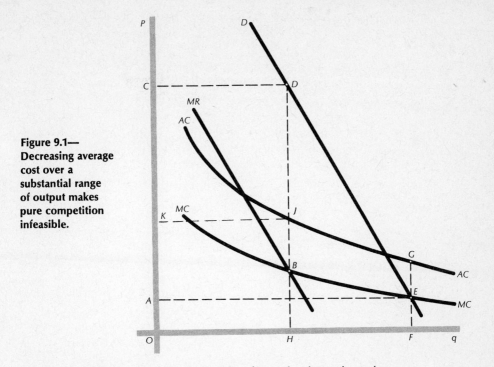

Figure 9.1—Decreasing average cost over a substantial range of output makes pure competition infeasible.

The possibilities open for oligopoly obviously depend on how sharply the average cost curve is decreasing and also on the elasticity of demand. If the average cost curve is declining slowly, as in Figure 9.1, then a larger number of firms could conceivably be supported at a profit, even though none of them are perfectly efficient. A quite common situation is depicted in Figure 9.2, where the average-cost

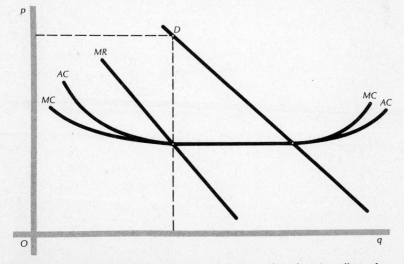

Figure 9.2—Minimum efficient size as a proportion of market size affects the feasibility of competition.

121

curve declines at relatively low levels of output, then remains roughly constant over a large part of the relevant length. In such industries technology sets a minimum scale for efficient operation which permits a fair number of firms to exist without hindering efficiency as a result of their size. Where average cost declines sharply over the relevant length, monopoly seems the most likely product.

As was suggested above, a large minimum efficient scale of plant explains the high degree of concentration in some industries. However, it is probably true that in most oligopolies in the United States a number of the firms in each industry are substantially larger than minimum efficient plant size would suggest. Two other aspects of sales efficiency are relevant here. These are economies of scale accruing to the firm rather than to the plant. For example there may be some cost savings to be made by establishing a national distribution organization which funnels the goods from the factories to the retailers in the most efficient manner. Another economy of scale may come from the requirements of advertising. Being able to mount a national campaign, given the availability of national media, such as magazines, television networks, and the like, offers the opportunity for more effective canvassing of consumers per dollar spent. These economies, too, probably do not suffice to explain the existing size of major oligopolistic enterprises.

A somewhat different consideration has to do with the relation between size and survival. The analogy here is with gamblers. Suppose two men are playing some fair game whose expected value is zero. Each bets a dollar at a time. One man brought $5 with him, the other $50. For the first man to go broke requires a much smaller string of bad luck than for the second. For example, the probability is .91 that the first man will go broke, but only .09 that this will happen to the second, assuming they play until one or the other event happens. Though the situation is not quite as rigid for an enterprise, the same sort of consideration applies. If banks are contracting credit it is the smaller and riskier firms that will be the first to be refused. And once they get into difficulties it becomes harder instead of easier to borrow. Thus the risk of ruin is substantially greater for the smaller firm.

One final aspect of size in oligopoly. For reasons we will discuss later there is a good deal of new product competition in many oligopoly industries. That is, many oligopolistic firms are seeking new products to manufacture and sell. The search for these opportunities takes a certain amount of staff, which the smallest firms probably could not support. More important, when an opportunity presents itself the firm will want to move quickly. This means ready access to finance which, as we have seen, is the readier the larger the firm—at least up to some point. So for yet another reason firms in these industries tend to be larger than considerations of efficient scale of production dictate.

We have suggested a number of reasons why oligopoly structure tends to develop in many industries. However, we have not yet looked at the other part of the problem. Why don't oligopolies become monopolies? It certainly appears to be in their interest to do so if they are profit maximizers, for we have already seen that the monopolist is in a position to extract maximum profits from an industry. It would seem to be profitable for the oligopolists to merge.

Probably in the United States the major reason they do not is that if they did they would be subject in most cases to immediate antitrust action. It is not at all clear just at what point during a process of concentration of ownership in an industry the government will step in to prevent further concentration—and be supported in its attempt by the courts. But the threat is constantly there and has a substantial effect on the behavior of oligopolists.

But many oligopolies exist in countries which do permit concentration to continue as long as the participants desire and whose courts will enforce market-sharing and even profits-pooling agreements. Also, the United States government is not perfectly consistent in its opposition to monopoly; indeed it would be very difficult for it to be so. First there is the grant of patents to the developers of new ideas in the realm of technology; patents are limited monopolies, giving the holder the exclusive right to exploit the invention for a period of years—usually seventeen. And even where patents are not at issue the first producer of a new product is for a while at least a monopolist. Obviously it would not be desirable for the government to pursue monopoly wherever and whenever it found it. The prospect of even a temporary monopoly can be an important stimulant to efforts to develop new products.

The above considerations point to a second and very important reason for the frequency of occurrence of oligopoly. Throughout the twentieth century, technology has been in a state of very rapid change. Many of these changes are commercially exploitable. The monopolist who is first to bring out a successful new product often has very limited ability to prevent competitors from entering his market. New processes are not always effectively covered by patents, and often effective substitutes can be found for the new processes and new products. Thus in a sense many oligopoly structures have emerged from an initial, short-run, and highly unstable monopoly. How much farther they will evolve of course depends on considerations like those we have already discussed. In manufacturing it seems that size considerations often prevent further evolution toward less concentrated structures.

Enough has been said by now to suggest that oligopoly is a very important form of market structure and, given continuation of existing American legal institutions, is likely to remain so for the near future. The question as to how close oligopolies are to monopoly price and just how their policies develop and are applied has still to be discussed. This is a complex subject about which economists do not yet have firm general conclusions. However, some insight into the range of possibilities can be helpful in giving the reader a feel for the oligopolist's attitudes and behavior.

Because no generalizations can really be made about *all* oligopoly behavior and because of the complexity of the issues, we will use only numerical examples to illustrate interaction between oligopolists. Also we will assume that there are only two oligopolists who count. Other firms in the industry follow the lead of these two, perhaps because these are the giants of the industry. Our procedure will be to assign payoffs—profits—to each oligopolist over some time period. The payoff depends in each case on two factors: the choice among his alternatives of each oligopolist.

Table 9.1

		B	
		Set monopoly price and stay there (M)	Accept monopoly price— secret price cutting (S)
A	Set monopoly price and stay there (M)	$+1, +1$	$-2, +1\frac{1}{2}$
	Accept monopoly price— secret price cutting (S)	$+1\frac{1}{2}, -2$	$-1, -1$

Table 9.1 shows the payoffs for one oligopoly situation. Each participant has two choices. The first alternative, M, is to move to the monopoly price and to stay there. This will lead to maximum industry profits, provided both oligopolists choose to do it. The payoffs in this case are shown in the upper left-hand box. Payoffs to oligopolist A are always shown first, the payoff to B second in each box, after the comma. The payoff is plus one (perhaps meaning a million dollars a year in profits) to each participant, so they are sharing the market equally.

Each participant has a second alternative, S. This is to indicate acceptance of the monopoly price, perhaps by printing it in his price lists, but then to engage in secret price cutting in an attempt to woo customers away from the competition. Each oligopolist can choose either alternative freely and without dependence on what his competitor does—though of course it make a difference in his income statement for the year. The four boxes of Table 9.1 show the payoffs to each oligopolist when each of the possible outcomes occur.

The payoffs are such that each participant has a maximum incentive to cheat, that is to appear to accept the agreement and then to attempt secretly to cut prices. The payoffs suggest that consumers have very little brand loyalty. Perhaps because the products are not differentiated at all or perhaps because the products of both firms are generally believed to be of comparable high quality. Hence if one firm engages in price cutting he substantially increases his sales to the point at which, despite the fact that he is selling below the monopoly price, he is able to make more profits than he would as a fifty-fifty sharer in industry maximum profits. This has a comparably negative effect on profits in the other firm as the upper right and lower left boxes show.

In this situation it seems almost certain that each participant will choose his second alternative S, even though as a result each firm will be getting the next to lowest profits possible.

> ► *An alternative is said to dominate another alternative if the payoff to the dominant alternative is greater than to the others regardless of the choice made by an opponent.*

In Table 9.1 for each participant alternative S dominates alternative M. For example, if A chooses S, he will get one-half more than if he had chosen M, given that B chooses M. And given that B chooses S, A loses one less by choosing S than if he chooses M. So regardless of B's behavior, it is beneficial for A to choose S. Since the payoffs to A and B are symmetrical, the same line of argument applies to B.

Let us consider two or three possible criteria that A might use in making his choice. One possibility is for him to assume that B is both smart and mean. If A is right, then B, regardless of his own welfare, will anticipate A's choice successfully and will choose the alternative which gives A the least profits. In such a situation A's best bet clearly is to choose the alternative whose maximum loss is as low as possible. This dictates alternative S as the choice. It is generally called the minimax criterion since it requires minimization of the maximum loss possible.[1]

Another way of looking at this game is to assume that the opponent's choice is not certain but that he will choose each alternative randomly with some given probability. A participant must first estimate the probability of his opponent choosing each alternative and then select the alternative that maximizes his own gain. This criterion maximizes the expected value of the outcome to the participant, as-

---

1. This criterion makes somewhat more sense in what are called zero sum games, that is, in games in which each participant's loss is the opponent's gain, so that the algebraic sum of gains and losses in each cell adds up to zero. Then it is enough to assume that your opponent is smart and is seeking his own gain rather than your destruction, to make the minimax criterion a good one. He does not also have to be mean.

suming of course that he has made a correct estimate of the probabilities. However, in our example it is not necessary to estimate the probabilities. Because alternate S dominates alternative M, each player chooses S regardless of the probabilities of his opponent's choice.

The results seem rather unsatisfactory. Is there no way that two oligopolists can get together and produce a better outcome than −1 to each? Of course there are some conceivable possibilities. Suppose each oligopolist is a gentleman who keeps his word. In this case he has to be a very special sort of gentleman, for in fact he is forbidden by law to give his word to a competitor to observe any price agreement. So this is not a very realistic assumption.

Consider another possibility. Suppose that it is very difficult to keep price cutting secret. Suppose also that there are grave dangers to an open price war. If each oligopolist fears that price cutting will lead to open price war and that prices will plummet as a result he may be reluctant to engage in secret price cutting. However, all this implies that the payoffs attaching to alternatives for both competitors have been wrong and should be given much larger negative numbers. We are talking about a different case that that depicted in Table 9.1.

So it appears that the solution [s, s]—i.e., alternative S chosen by each oligopolist—is a very likely and stable outcome given our assumptions. The solution could apply only to a situation in which it is possible to engage in a considerable amount of price cutting without running much risk of being found out by competitors. This situation is likely to occur, for example, when the price cutting can be confined to a relatively small number of large-scale buyers of the oligopoly's product. It is also likely to occur when an oligopolist has an interest in one or more of the buying companies.

Table 9.2

		B	
		(M)	(S)
A	M	$+1, +1$	$-2, +\frac{1}{2}$
	S	$+\frac{1}{2}, -2$	$-1\frac{1}{2}, -1\frac{1}{2}$

Table 9.2 depicts a slightly different situation. Again there is not much brand loyalty so that secret price cutting will work. However, demand is less elastic so that the gains from price cutting are less; the firm that engages in it alone cannot recoup his share of the joint monopoly profits, and if both firms engage in it the outcome is somewhat less satisfactory than in the Table 9.1 situation.

A minimaxer will still choose alternative S in this case. However, S no longer dominates M, so the choice using expected values is no longer clear, again assuming confident estimates of the probabilities can be made. Note that if A is certain that B will choose S, then he, too, will choose S and that if he is certain that B will choose M, then he will choose M himself. If the expectations criterion is used by both participants and if each thinks the other is likely to choose M with a probability of more than one-half, then he, too, will choose it; but even though the highest returns to each are in this box, there is no assurance that it will be the outcome.

One more point about Table 9.2. Once the two oligopolists reach tacit agreement that M is the best alternative, neither will have an incentive to leave it in order to improve his own situation. It is the fear of loss represented by the -2 payoff, not the lure of gain that puts difficulties in the way of obtaining monopoly profits in this case. Hence the choice of the minimaxer.

These two examples have grossly oversimplified the complexities of the situations in which oligopolists find themselves. We have assumed that there are only two alternatives and two firms and that the payoffs are perfectly symmetrical for each participant. Even so, our examples perhaps will suffice to suggest a few conclusions about oligopoly:

1. It is by no means clear that oligopolies, even those consisting of only a handful of firms, can manage to achieve the monopoly profit situation. Much depends on the structure of demand and cost and on the number and nature of the buyers of the product. Consequently it is very difficult to generalize about pricing under oligopoly.

2. The less certain are the actions and reactions of competitors the harder it is to avoid relatively unpleasant outcomes. This suggests that rational oligopolists will seek ways of increasing their confidence in the reactions of competitors. One perfectly legal way to do this is to standardize information about the state of the market, the methods of costing in the industry, and current price lists of members. Through trade associations, organizations sponsored and financed by members of an industry, such information can be collected and made available to members. For example, this will make it easier for one member to have some confidence that his estimate of, say, just where the monoply price is, is shared at least roughly by his competitors. Plenty of uncertainty remains, but the ubiquitousness of trade associations suggests that their informational functions are highly valued by members. Their publications may also serve to send up trial balloons about possible reactions to changing market situations, for example by publishing speeches of leaders of the industry describing these changes and hinting at appropriate reactions.

3. The unavoidability of a considerable amount of uncertainty about rival reactions—not to mention the question as to how accurately the payoffs of alternative actions can be estimated in advance

—suggests that oligopoly prices may be somewhat sticky or resistant to changing market conditions. But though this is frequently the case our examples also suggest that there will be exceptions to this rule. The situation of Table 9.1 can easily remain unstable over a considerable period of time with continued attempts to make the monopoly price stick and continued resort to price cutting by one or another of the participants.

4. Because of both the informational uncertainties and the interactions among participants it is virtually impossible to define unequivocally what constitutes profit-maximizing behavior. However, we may point to one possibly misleading aspect of the oligopolist's behavior. Oligopolists seem frequently to engage in very keen product competition—that is, in attempts to develop and market new products which will expand their firm's share of the market for a class of products. Sometimes these products differ from one another in little more than the nature of the advertising campaign used to promote them; in recent years cigarettes are probably a notable case in point. In other cases the products do differ substantially, as with the introduction of stainless-steel razor blades or engine-in-rear automobiles. But the emphasis on expanding market share has suggested that these oligopolists are more interested in growth than in profits, and that because of the flow of new products they are somehow more "progressive" than firms in industries with a different market structure.

The discussion to date suggests that because oligopoly contains such diverse possibilities generalizations like this are out of place. A stable, monopoly-price, little-product-development oligopoly is perfectly possible. Alternatively, so is one in which there is price stability at or near the monopoly level, but in which product differentiation and large-scale advertising campaigns reduce net profit levels to enterprises to a level well below that of monopoly. This behavior tends to divert substantial resources into promotion efforts which have little effect on industry demand, but which essentially serve the purpose of defending each firm's existing market share against competitive encroachment. In still other cases product competition may take the more progressive form of substantial new developments, of useful consumer goods and services.

Finally, oligopolists need not always compete with the same firm in their product development programs. If the situation in one or several product markets has become relatively stabilized, opportunities for increasing profits may be limited, with respect to these goods, to picking up a roughly constant share of a slowly growing market. The oligopolist may now turn his attention to entry possibilities in quite a diverse variety of other markets in his search for expanding profits. The growth and profit incentives may well coincide. A by-product of this kind of search may be to increase the competitiveness of markets whose current producers recognize the threat of entry that constantly exists from such powerful potential competitors. And of course the entry decision itself will be made only after a careful assessment of the implications of current market structure and prospects. Obviously a rapidly growing market is much more attractive and less dangerous to enter than a tightly knit, stable oligopoly with slowly growing demand. Empirical studies have suggested that persistently higher-than-average profit rates are much more common in industries in which four or five firms are dominant than in industries where more than eight firms share the limelight. This seems reasonable enough, provided due weight is given to the variety of possible outcomes under conditions of oligopoly bargaining.

In a number of situations two large, more or less monopolistic organizations face one another across the market as sole buyer and seller of some product. This case of bilateral or two-sided monopoly involves many of the considerations of the oligopoly case we have been discussing. Again the range of solutions is substantial. But one or two of the possible variations are worth a comment.

Across-the-Market Bargaining

Let us suppose to start with that the two organizations are both businesses. In Figure 9.3, three possible outcomes under different circumstances are shown. Had there been competition on both sides of the market the price-output combination would occur at the

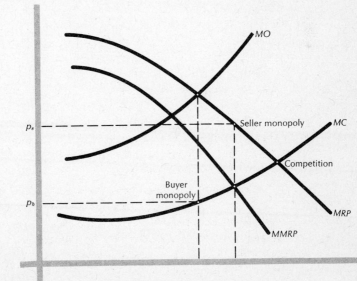

Figure 9.3—Monopoly on both sides of the market.

intersection of marginal-cost and marginal-revenue-product curves. If the buyer of the product alone were a monopolist and the sellers competitive, he would take account of his ability to influence price, would draw up the marginal-outlay curve as described in Chapter 8, and would choose the output determined by the intersection of marginal outlay and marginal-revenue product curves and take his price from the marginal-cost curve. A third possibility is precisely the reverse: the seller holds a monopoly of sales and the buyers are competitive. Then price effects are described by a curve marginal to the marginal-revenue product curve and the much higher priced seller-monopoly equilibrium would occur as depicted on the diagram.

We do not have enough information to say much of anything about the price-output agreement if there is monopoly on both sides of the market. One might think that at least the range of possible price variation is set by the buyer-and-seller-monopoly prices. However, even this is not the case. In the short run a very powerful firm might even be able to force a very weak firm to accept a price-output deal which entailed losses. Furthermore each side is likely to try to conceal information relating to its true cost and revenue curves so as to mislead the opponent in the appropriate direction. These are the two common features of bargaining situations: (1) economic data are insufficient to determine the profit-maximizing outcome; and (2) the incentive to distort information is strong.

Since so little can be said in general about the result in this situation, let us turn to somewhat more specific examples. Suppose first that the supplier is an industrial union which has organized all the production laborers in an industry and that the buyer is the trade association of the industry, which has been authorized to serve as bargaining agent for the individual firms in an oligopolistic industry. This is a case in which it is possible that the supplier will not bargain over the amount of labor to be supplied but only over price. In this case the buyer can be assured of lying on his marginal revenue product whatever the price. However, the buyer no longer faces a supply curve, nor has he any clear idea as to what terms will be acceptable to the union. Of course the association can make some rough assessment of the financial resources of the union and may have some insight into the mood of the workers. But it is hard to translate this into a set of feasible (acceptable) points on the diagram. Nor does the union have an incentive to tell the association exactly what it will find acceptable. The union will hope by exaggerating the militancy of its members to frighten the association into a better settlement.

And of course the reverse situation is also true. The association does not want to tip off the union in advance as to what it considers an acceptable settlement, but hopes to bargain the union down by perhaps providing a gloomy picture of market prospects, costs, and the like. The members of the association will be reluctant to supply much public information about aspects of their operations which might be of use to the union in bargaining sessions. Thus each side has an incentive to conceal and distort its own situation and also an incentive to find out as much as possible about the true state of affairs of the opponent. Informationally, therefore, the bilateral monopoly situation differs substantially from oligopoly.[2]

In union-management bargaining the amount of labor to be taken by management is often a matter of concern to the union. In this case an attempt may be made to force managament off its marginal revenue product curve. Work rules and featherbedding and safety rules may be means to this as well as other ends.

Another common bilateral monopoly situation pits government as purchaser of goods against a large business. In the case of certain kinds of military and space equipment there may be only one or two prospective suppliers and only one important buyer, so the bilateral monopoly situation is closely approximated. However, there is another way in which this situation may be approximated, even though there are many possible suppliers. A common government procurement practice is to draw up specifications for the good in question and then ask for bids from private firms for delivery of some fixed amount. Each interested firm submits a sealed bid and the bids are opened and made public by the government procurement agent on the appointed date. This sounds like a practice designed to induce competitive bidding. However, for an oligopolized industry the effect may be just the opposite: the government's procedure may serve to encourage collusion, tacit or otherwise, because it eliminates the possibility of secret price cutting. The result may be a situation closely resembling bilateral monopoly.

Both sides may have powerful hands in this bargaining situation. The government can reject all bids, can threaten to buy the goods abroad, can threaten direct intervention through price control, or can threaten to take other government business elsewhere. As the repository of national coercive action as well as the largest buyer of a great many goods, all these threats may be quite effective. However, industry, too, is not without resources. Local congressmen are likely

---

2. In the case of secret price cutting, one firm had an incentive to keep its price cutting secret, but in the interest of market stability this firm may be willing to provide much detailed information about other aspects of its operation to the trade association. Other firms in the industry, who are trying to maintain the official price, have a strong incentive to provide accurate information. In the bilateral monopoly just described both parties have strong incentives to distort information. But this is not always true; for example, if the range of acceptable alternatives to one party is really very narrow, and improvement in the terms is not so important to that party as getting the minimum acceptable agreement. One must never forget the complexity and variety of bargaining situations.

to be sympathetic to calls for help; and the idea that some moderate level of profits is only fair will have considerable appeal in Washington. Again each party has a strong incentive to find out as much as possible about the other while conveying as little as possible in the way of accurate information about its own state of affairs.

However, this sort of mutual misleading cannot be tolerated in many of the more crucial areas of government procurement, and especially with respect to the development of new products of importance to the military and space programs. For this reason, among others, a variety of types of special contracts have been developed to make mutual trust and information exchange an incentive on both sides. Among the most interesting of these is the so-called incentive contract. In this case the government may select in advance a single firm and propose that the two parties work out a contract for development of some new product such as a long-range rocket. The government offers to pay the costs of contract development, which may be a matter of millions of dollars, whether or not ultimate agreement is reached. Then both sides work together in specifying what has to be done and in making estimates of the costs involved for each step. The final contract will specify completion dates and performance characteristics for each of the work packages that make up the final product. Performance according to contract is rewarded, and if certain kinds of performance are exceeded, bonus payments are awarded. The company thus may get widely varying profits out of the contract depending on its ability to perform up to or better than the specifications. This sort of contract by no means eliminates the bargaining element from the situation, but it does serve to expand somewhat the area of mutual interest: both sides now want a first rate product at as low a cost as possible. And the bargaining is largely confined to the early stage of contract development. Though far from a panacea, it represents a considerable improvement over the cost-plus-fixed-fee contract which has been a standard feature of contracting in this area in the past and frequently has led to underestimation of costs in the contract by severalfold.

Bargaining and Market Adjustment

In many markets there appears to be little or no bargaining. A large number of buyers may be faced with a price that they consider to be unalterable in the short run; they must either take the product or leave it at that price. The suppliers of the good fix the price and if excess supply or demand shows up they adjust the price accordingly.

However, a great deal of bargaining does go on during the process of price adjustment in many, perhaps in most, markets. The fact that Oriental-bazaar type haggling over the prices of relatively minor purchases has largely disappeared from the American retail trading scene should not mislead as to this fact. It should always be remembered that the market is not a machine; if a price changes, someone has to do the changing. If the price has not changed recently, the changer is betting against the market that the going price is no longer an equilibrium price. As we have seen in the discussion of oligopoly, the mere fact that someone has changed the price of the good may in fact turn an equilibrium price into a disequilibrium price. Whenever this happens there is an element of bargaining in the adjustment process.

The markets in which bargaining is most likely to occur are those in which it is difficult to identify an equilibrium price. The auction of rare goods provides an example. The fact that they are rare means than an individual item is not likely frequently to be the object of a deal. Consequently it is not clear what the equilibrium price currently is. Of course some information is conveyed by the prices that roughly comparable objects have been drawing in the recent past. But the fact that a deal has been made does not mean that the deal was at the equilibrium price. A sizable penumbra surrounds the equilibrium price as bidding begins. A skillful dealer at a public auction can manipulate the process of bidding and the flow of information in an effort to change expectations of the bidders about the ultimate price, thus pushing the bidding above the price that a different flow of information and bids would produce. Clearly the bargaining element of misleading presentation of information occurs at many such auctions.

A market on which millions of deals involving consumers are made every year and which contains bargaining as an important element is the used-car market. The market adjustment is strongly influenced by the great variety of product qualities available and by considerable uncertainty as to the quality of any particular item. In addition the process of becoming informed is a costly one for the consumer. He can spend two or three days hunting and still not have a precise knowledge of the equilibrium prices for the range of cars in which he is interested. In most cities he will find that in fact this market is never in equilibrium in our formal sense of all deals for a car of given quality tending to be made at a single price. Instead there are dealers who tend to specialize in the "first-lot" buyers, who in effect are willing to pay a premium price to avoid a long search. Other dealers may specialize in providing cars of stable quality. They, too, charge a premium price and it is not always easy for the consumer to tell whether he is in the hands of the one or the other, even though they are in fact selling quite different products. When becoming informed is costly a market equilibrium is likely to consist of a range of prices which will persist over time and which in effect constitute an equilibrium price range.

Despite the element of misinforming that tends to enter into bargaining situations the process is often a useful one. By bargaining one is searching for information about the state of the market as well as the position of one's competitors on that market. One useful function it may serve is to reduce the number of nonequilibrium deals that are actually made. Where it is difficult to acquire information as to the results of deals struck in the recent past on a market, bargaining provides a sort of substitute for that information, acquired of course at a cost. By bargaining, one may avoid making a contract at the wrong price. Sometimes, too, the skillful dealer may be able by bargaining to identify potential dealers who may be willing to accept deals at better—from the point of view of the bargainer—than the equilibrium prices. The homeowner who sets his price a thousand dollars above the market and then waits until someone comes along who is willing to pay that price is an example of this sort of bargaining. Of course bargaining also has its dysfunctional side, especially if it produces so much misinformation about the state of the market that prices tend to move away from the equilibrium point. Examples of this have occurred, such as the famous South Sea Bubble of eighteenth-century England, and in more recent American real estate booms in which misleading information has created false expectations which have tended to cumulate into a speculative mania. Prices many times the longer-run equilibrium sometimes become the temporary equilibrium point of deals under such circumstances.

Complex products such as new businesses are especially difficult to price on a market. Here uncertainty is inevitably high and opportunities for misleading especially promising. In the case of smaller businesses many participants in the market may not have the resources or background necessary to make an effective appraisal of prospects and risks. The very high failure rates of small retail businesses suggest that the market for these types of new businesses has a very poorly organized information system.

However, there is another factor which enters into decision making under uncertainty and which may have a considerable effect on market adjustment processes when uncertainty is present. The fact is that we do not know exactly how to define rational behavior under risk. For example, consider the two criteria that were discussed above in connection with the oligopoly examples: minimaxing and the expectation criterion. We did not deal with the former in a probabilistic context but the criterion can be made to apply to the same situations in which the expectation criterion was applied. Which of these criteria ought a profit-maximizing businessman to use in his decision making? To some extent the answer depends on his attitude toward risk. But what should his attitude toward risk be? It is not clear that risk aversion is bad or that shooting the works on a long shot is a poor choice. Nor is it clear that attitudes toward risk are built into the personality and so are to be taken as given by the economist. This is all the more true when the probabilities that enter into the situation are not firmly established but are based on a more or less subjective evaluation of the situation.

Finally it should be noted that the study of probabilistic choice is not a part of the universal education given to all Americans, much less to all the world's businessmen. Because of the nonintuitive nature of the properties of many risky situations, it may be that the rules of thumb used by many of us are quite inexpedient. One possible instance of this has been studied by psychologists and found to be a very common practice. It is called *probability matching*. Suppose, for example, that a number of people are placed in an experimental situation in which they are to call to the experimenter whether, in a series of flashes, the next flash will be red or green. They are given no information as to the frequency with which this will occur. The subjects are paid a reward proportional to the number of right guesses. Experimenters have discovered that if they arrange the signals so that, without following a pattern from one flash to the next, the red, say, comes up on the average three times out of four, the subjects will gradually come to understand this. Once they have recognized that red flashes more often than green, the way for them to maximize their reward is to call red every time. But few subjects in fact do this. Instead they match their calls to the probability, tending to call red in this case, after the first few trials, about three times out of four.

Is this irrational behavior in the sense that, if they understood the laws of probability better, the subjects would adopt the profit-maximizing approach? Not necessarily. It may be that they fear that if they call red every time the experimenter will switch the odds on them. That is, they may have a somewhat fearful attitude toward the world —probability matching occurs in quite a wide variety of situations— and in effect are bargaining with nature (the experimenter in our case) by accepting a more modest gain than the maximum possible. But students who have some training in statistics are less likely to engage in probability matching. The point of all this is that market adjustments may be slow and may come to a halt before an equilibrium price is reached for a variety of reasons, one of which may be the inexpedient attitudes of many of the participants.

At the beginning of this chapter the question was raised as to whether in imperfect markets the outcomes tended to approximate competition or monopoly more closely. We cannot attempt an empirical answer to this question. However, an analytic point is in order. The profits test has been proposed as an answer to this question. If a particular class of markets typically has persistently higher profits than the average rates and this cannot be attributed reasonably to the quality of the management, this class of markets does seem to be coming rather closer to the monopoly side of market structure. As was mentioned earlier, this does occur with many highly concentrated oligopolies in the United States.

However, the converse situation is much harder to evaluate. The fact that a class of markets does not persistently tend to develop profits in excess of the average may reflect a variety of factors other than a near-competitive efficiency of resource allocation. In an oligopoly it may be the product of very intensive product differentiation and promotion which does little or nothing for consumer satisfaction. Or it may reflect the poorly organized informational system of the market, with much bargaining and/or nonequilibrium deals absorbing time and energy and promoting considerable misallocation of resources. Or the informational poverty of the market may not represent a malallocation of resources but the unavoidable technical properties of the product, and the low profit rates may be a result of keen competition under conditions of easy entry. The empirical evaluation of market performance is an extremely tricky and not yet well-developed branch of economics.

10

The Market System

In the preceding chapters we have been dealing primarily with the behavior of individual decision units and of groups of decision units acting in a single market. This approach is called partial equilibrium analysis. It is "equilibrium" analysis because it concentrates attention on a special class of situations, namely those which, once attained, will tend to continue to have the same properties until underlying data change. It is "partial" analysis because it concentrates attention on at most one market and assumes that things remain unchanged in the rest of the economy during the course of adjustments within the market under discussion. This approach is a useful way of organizing our knowledge about market behavior, but it leaves a great deal of such behavior out of account, and can be quite misleading, as the discussion of the labor market in Chapter 8 showed. Consequently a more complex form of analysis has been developed, called general equilibrium analysis, to deal with the effects of interaction among markets.

In this chapter we will look at the economy from the point of view of general equilibrium analysis. Actually, however, there are at least two ways of viewing general equilibrium analysis. The first is the familiar perspective of a model, of a set of specific assumptions about the way a group of markets work and of the implications of these assumptions. As may be anticipated, general equilibrium models are complex affairs whose description requires mathematical formulation which cannot be very usefully encapsuled in a diagram or two. What we can do is give a brief verbal description of such a model and describe some of its conclusions. What we already know about individual markets will tend to lend plausibility to many of these conclusions, but the conclusions cannot be demonstrated here. The second point of view might be called, following the language of the late Joseph Schumpeter, that of vision rather than of models. The model of general equilibrium is itself part of an even more general vision or way of looking at the economic system which most economists have in common. Many factors which are not yet integrated into general equilibrium models have been partially explored and are known to have important consequences for the way in which an economy works. In the economist's vision of the economic system the model of general equilibrium occupies a vital place but is a kind of partial analysis at a higher level of complexity than single-market partial analysis. The vision does not produce demonstrable conclusions. Instead it provides insight as to important factors that might be missed if the vision is ignored. Because many factors tend to be operating to influence an economy at any point in time, it is important to become aware of these factors even though the precise nature of their impact on the economy is not yet known.

In this chapter we will try to provide a vision of the market system. We begin with a particular case of economic interaction in which the distinction between partial and general analysis is exposed in an especially clear light. Then we will organize the discussion of the factors influencing the market system under five headings. First will come some properties of the general equilibrium model. This is followed by the processes by which market systems adjust to changes in the environment and to disequilibrium situations. Then comes the information system of the market economy. Fourth comes the nature of the incentives which markets generate and, finally, the creativity stimulated by the market system and the creativity of the system itself, its self-repairing features. This vision should provide us with some perspective as to the kinds of things a market system does well and the ways in which failure or at least relatively poor performance may result from its operation.

Market Interactions: an Example
In 1860 cotton textile manufacture was one of England's major industries. About four fifths of the raw cotton used in English factories was imported from the United States. With the outbreak of the Civil War in the United States, American cotton became virtually unobtain-

able in England as a result of the Federal blockade of southern ports. Economic historians have developed a considerable body of information about the effects of this sudden and very sharp downward shift in the supply of an important input on the English economy over the next three or four years.

The direct economic impact of scarcity should be an increase in the price of cotton. This, too, was sharp: by 1864 the English price was nearly four times its prewar level. At that price the amount of cotton demanded was much lower, which in turn led to a much lower derived demand for workers in the textile industry. So the wages of cotton textile workers fell.

Since other fabrics can be substituted for cotton in consumption, the derived demand for flax and linen rose and on consumer markets the price of linen goods rose substantially. Many cotton textile workers migrated to areas in which these rival fabrics were being produced. In Lancashire, the center of cotton textile manufacture, the sharp decline in profits and wages led to a decrease in demand for consumer goods in general, so that shopkeepers in the area were hard hit also.

And so forth. All through the English economy the market system transmitted the consequences of this sharp exogenous change in market conditions. It is this interrelatedness among markets of all kinds that is the central concern of general equilibrium analysis. The impacts in this particular case can be traced quite far, and in some cases the magnitude of the impact estimated quantitatively, because the initial impact came from outside the English market system and involved a product vital to the English economy. In most cases there are a number of changes occurring simultaneously so that causation is much harder to trace. But the Cotton Famine provides a striking example of the kinds of interactions the general equilibrium analysis is designed to cope with.

General equilibrium, like its partial counterpart, has the property that once achieved, and in the absence of change in any of the underlying data, it will continue indefinitely. In a competitive market, if the market has produced a single price such that supply and demand are equal, and each firm finds that its marginal cost is just equal to that price, and all households are at their maximum satisfaction points, then the market is in equilibrium. In the general equilibrium model this must be true for all markets. It will also apply to capital markets, so that the interest rate calls forth exactly the amount of resources for investment as are demanded at that interest rate by consumers of those resources (investors). Factor markets, too, are in equilibrium, with the factor price calling forth an offer of the factor

General Equilibrium

which just equals the derived demand, while firms demanding the factor find that the amount they are taking has the property that the marginal revenue product just equals the factor price.

If all these markets are competitive, and tastes and technology are appropriate, then, as we saw in Chapter 7, the economy is in a state of Pareto optimality. This means that no alteration in the production and/or exchange of goods can improve the satisfaction of some consumers and factor suppliers without decreasing the satisfaction of some others. This is the central efficiency proposition for the competitive market system. However, it should be noted that it implies some other, less all-embracing notions of efficiency. For example each decision unit in the economy has, in a state of over-all Pareto optimality, reached a point in which it, individually, cannot improve its position at the given market prices by changing its pattern of purchases and sales. Also it implies that each market is cleared: inventories are neither being piled up nor drawn down. Considering that market systems may have millions of markets for distinguishable goods and tens of millions of participants, this would be a really remarkable achievement.

However, even so, the general equilibrium of a market economy may not be a particularly desirable state of affairs. There are three important ways in which a market equilibrium may not produce an ideal state of affairs—and two of these apply to a competitive equilibrium.

The first failure has to do with the distribution of wealth. The market system may produce a great variety of equilibrium states depending on the distribution of ownership of valuable assets among members of the society. Some differences are obvious: for example, if wealth is highly concentrated, the equilibrium demand for large yachts will be much higher than if it is spread widely among households. More importantly, in the absence of a large middle class, demand for consumer durables may make mass production of these items infeasible, which might have dramatic consequences on the life styles of housewives as well as the demand for domestic servants. However, it should also be noted that very high concentrations of wealth are probably inconsistent with the existence of competitive markets. The very wealthy must get their wealth ultimately from some form of productive activity, in particular from the ownership of enterprises. Thus high concentration of wealth suggests that there will also be some concentration of ownership which in turn will be inconsistent with competition. Thus the range of distributions of wealth which is consistent with competitive equilibrium may not be so very great. However, a great variety of differences in the possible lists of the names of the wealthy is certainly possible.

A second way in which competitive equilibrium may be undesirable stems from the technical structure of the economy rather than
from wealth distribution or organization. The concept of external
effects has already been defined: it is direct interaction in the satisfactions of households or the production functions of enterprises, or
both. If a factory produces noxious smoke that makes eyes water in
neighboring residences, there is no obvious market mechanism by
which the producer of the smoke can be made to compensate the
inconvenienced householders. And without having to pay for this
"cost" he imposes on households, the owner of the factory has no
market incentive (other than possible effects on the productivity of
his own workers) to look for a less "costly" production process.
Whenever externalities like this occur, the market equilibrium ceases
to be Pareto optimal. For example, it might be possible to make
everyone in the neighborhood better off if the households were to
pay for the installation of a smoke-control device on the factory
smokestack. But the households can find no organized market in
which they can buy smoke diminution, so that this improvement
does not occur as the result of market action.

A third way in which a market equilibrium may be undesirable
is if it is not a competitive equilibrium. If some markets are monopolized they are still cleared and all participants have done as well as
they can at the going market prices. The monopolists have chosen the
market prices for their goods in order to maximize their profits. This,
as we have seen, means that fewer of their goods are produced than
would be produced under competition, a result which is not Pareto
optimal.

To achieve an equilibrium is a considerable accomplishment for
a complex economy. But even if we are assured that market economies are generally at or close to equilibrium, these three special
situations show that we may not necessarily find the resulting answers
to the questions of What, How, and For Whom to be particularly
desirable or even tolerable.

The single-market adjustment process described in earlier chapters has participants responding to excess supply by reducing price
and to excess demand by increasing price. This was shown in the
usual case of downward-sloping demand curve and upward-sloping
supply curve to tend to move the price toward the equilibrium position. The general equilibrium model consists of a collection of such
markets which may be in disequilibrium and so under the influence
of the same tendency to move toward equilibrium. However, there is
a complication. What happens in one market tends to affect what
happens in others. On our diagrams this shows up as a shift in one or
both of the curves. So the adjustment process in each market is com-

**Market
Adjustment
in the Model**

plicated by the shifts that occur in supply and demand curve as a result of changes occurring in other markets which are also in the process of adjustment.

The most important thing to note about this process is that the tendency to move toward equilibrium in each market, given the supply and demand curves, remains unchanged. This creates a strong direct pressure throughout the market system toward a general equilibrium. However, several factors may prevent this from occurring or from being completed.

The first possibility is that in some individual markets the equilibrium is not stable. An example of this is shown in Figure 10.1. Here

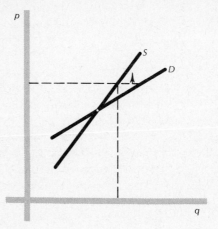

Figure 10.1—An unstable market.

the demand curve is upward-sloping, indicating that the market is operating in the range in which this good is strongly inferior to some other one, so much so that the demand curve has a positive slope less than that of the supply curve. As a result the market will not respond to a disturbance by returning to equilibrium. For example, if the initial price yields excess demand the reaction of increasing price will tend to create still greater excess demand, and the new price will be farther from equilibrium than the initial price.

Another example of a single market that does not come to equilibrium illustrates the so-called cobweb effect, and is shown in Figure 10.2. Suppose farmers set their output levels for this year on the basis of last year's prices, since they must decide how much land to put into this crop at the planting season, some months in advance of harvest and sale of the crop on the market. That is, the amount supplied to the market this period depends on the price farmers received last period. Suppose also that initially they guess badly, perhaps because demand has shifted out to the right. Thus, assuming a price of p_0 in Figure 10.2, farmers plant S_1 of corn. But this amount will be taken,

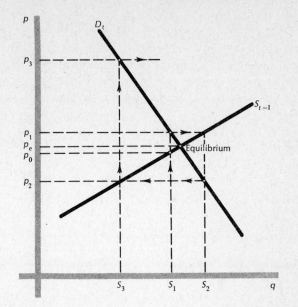

Figure 10.2—The cobweb, a lagged market adjustment mechanism.

assuming no carryover of corn from one year to the next, at price p_1 as determined by the demand curve, DD. In the following year this price p_1 dictates supply S_2, which is farther from the equilibrium than was S_1. In the third year supply S_3, based on price p_2, deviates still further from equilibrium. Thus the corn market seems to be "exploding," with price and output deviating farther from the equilibrium value with each new crop. Note that after the first year neither the supply nor demand curve shifts. It is the lagged reaction of farmers to market conditions, particularly price, that causes this result; also the demand curve is steeper than the supply curve. This, too, is necessary if the market is to be unstable. Finally note that if this market once gets to the equilibrium point it will tend to stay there until one of the curves shifts.

The first of these two types of single-market instability apparently is very rare; indeed there does not appear to be a single empirically substantiated case. The second may be more common, especially in its milder form of a substantial delay in reaching equilibrium as a result of lag-induced oscillations about the equilibrium point. In general, however, one would not be inclined to have serious doubts about market-system stability on grounds such as these.

A second kind of instability occurs when a set of markets, each of which is stable by itself, is unstable as a result of mutual interaction. Such markets are interconnected in a variety of directions. For example, the price of bread may affect the demand for margarine and the price of butter the demand for bread. In addition the price of

bread may affect the demand for potatoes, and the demand for potatoes the demand for margarine (also used on potatoes). And the
prices of and demands for butter and margarine interact closely. In
addition there may be a number of still more indirect interconnections, all of which tend to shift the demand for butter when there is
a change in demand for bread. It is quite conceivable that for some
goods these indirectly and directly induced shifts in demand and supply may move the momentary equilibrium about so much as to induce
movements away from the equilibrium. Figure 10.3 shows such a case.

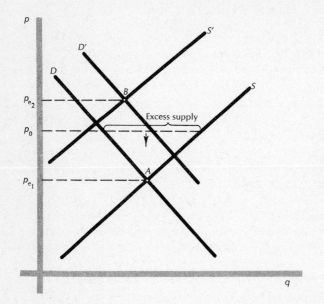

**Figure 10.3—How
multiple-market
instability might
work.**

Initially price is p_0 so that there is excess supply with respect to the
demand curves D and S. But the downward shift in price which the
excess supply induces also has effects in other markets which cause
a shift in supply and demand to D' and S'. This new equilibrium is
above p_0, so that the downward movement in price actually is a
movement away from the new equilibrium price p_{e_2}.

We know very little about the importance of adjustment interactions of this kind in practice. There is some presumption that if they
were widespread so that market economies were explosive in their
oscillations we would long since have shifted to some other kind
of economic system. However, it is also possible that there are sufficient frictions in the way market systems operate in practice that
these oscillations do not show up clearly. To these frictions and to
a somewhat less mechanical description of adjustment we now turn.

Of all the properties of the market system none is more striking than its ability to organize vast quantities of useful information for the making of millions of decisions by the various participants. The list of goods available and their prices are all the information any participant in a competitive equilibrium needs to know in order to make his own decisions efficiently. Armed with this information the individual household consults its own tastes and adjusts its budget expenditures according to the rule of equating the last dollar's worth of satisfaction from consuming each actually purchased good.[1] The firm consults its production possibilities and applies the competitive rules to adjusting outputs and inputs, given technology, and prices. And the markets themselves keep the equilibrium prices available as information to all comers. Thus each individual decision unit need collect only a minute fraction of the information available in order to make its own decisions. Considering the complexity of these various decisions it is no wonder that even highly authoritarian societies like the Soviet Union have tried to copy the decentralized market decision process for a large fraction of these decisions.

However, this idealized picture of the competitive equilibrium seriously understates the informational costs of achieving and sustaining equilibrium. For example, we have already discussed (in Chapters 3 and 9) the problem a market participant faces in deciding whether or not the price he is offered is an equilibrium price. If the purchase or sale is important to him he may decide to spend a significant portion of his current resources in resolving this issue, for example by searching among other potential deals. Another possibility is that the price, though currently an equilibrium price, may change in a favorable direction as a result of supply or demand shifts. In many markets there exist some expectations among the informed on such questions as this. But it is costly in time and resources to become informed, the more so the more complex or the less well organized is the market in question. These problems can be especially serious in markets which, for reasons already discussed, tend to produce a range of prices even in equilibrium.

There are a number of economic decisions in which the participant cannot be content with knowledge of his own technology or tastes. For example, a businessman considering an expansion of his plant should have at least some knowledge about the production techniques associated with current best practices in his industry. Typically he will also have to search a bit to see if there are not on the horizon new techniques not yet adopted anywhere in the indus-

1. The same rule is applied in considering alternative allocations of labor or other factor services offered by the household.

try, though perhaps already in use in other industries, which are ready for application to his own business. Clearly adequate knowledge for wise decisions about new plants in an industry whose technology is in a process of change can involve very complex and costly search and processing of information.

One can easily conceive of a market which is in a relatively stable equilibrium which is far from efficient because of the ignorance of participants. It is often argued that retail markets for many goods, and especially those which are produced under conditions of oligopoly, are very likely to be in this condition. One reason for this is the very limited capacity of many households to collect and process information. If no one in the family has much education and if incomes in the past have been low so that experience with market practices is very limited, a household may search over long periods of time among only a very limited set of alternatives, all of which are substantially different in their characteristics from those of the efficient consumption goods. Thus the poor may buy in a local corner market instead of the nearest supermarket, not because it is too costly to go to the supermarket but out of habit or even timidity. Inexperience and the resulting malleability of the household's head in the face of a skilled salesman may keep such a household from doing much searching even in the purchase of a major durable like an automobile.

Much the same thing may happen in the case of a small business. The owner is himself relatively inexperienced in dealings in many markets and has not the time or staff to acquire specialized information. This may lead him to waste resources by entering an industry when the market signals clearly say: Stay out! And even though his mistakes have the effect of raising his costs or of leading him to change to a price that does not maximize profits, he may still survive, at least in the short run, or even in the long run in an industry where a "competitive fringe" of small firms is tolerated by a stable oligopoly.

Another kind of ignorance can develop as a result of inadequacies of market organization. An ideal set of competitive capitalist markets will include a full set of futures markets, of markets which provide equilibrium expected prices for goods far into the future. These are necessary for decisions relating to the production of factories which will produce some of these future goods. They are also relevant for consumer budget allocations relating to the timing of purchase of consumer durables, including homes, and decisions about saving as opposed to spending. If there are few such markets, participants may of course still make their own estimates of the future prices. However, this is an imperfect substitute for the markets themselves, for the latter provide the arbitrage, the adjustment of differing expectations among potential and actual dealers by the usual market adjustment processes. Without the futures markets, equilibrium future prices cannot be established.

Another kind of information failure may be the result of educational deficiencies in the society. A consumer who has never been taught how to calculate interest rates or to understand the rudiments of compound interest may not be able to evaluate alternative credit offers by different finance companies. The same applies to the evaluation of risk. As was suggested in the last chapter, many participants, businessmen as well as consumers, may be so ignorant of the properties of risky situations that they cannot evaluate risky alternatives effectively, and may use rules of thumb that are quite inexpedient in serving their own goals.

Finally we may mention failures of the market mechanism itself, which may provide the wrong signals to participants, so that even though individuals act wisely the market leads them astray. Notable instances of this are monopoly and external effects. The monopolist prices his goods too high, not from his own point of view but from the point of view of Pareto optimality. Individual purchasers of the monopolist's product act wisely, taking the monopolist's price as given and adjusting their budgets accordingly. And no one has the information that would make everyone better off—namely, the information necessary to consummate the "big deal" by which the monopolist would be bought out by consumers and competition established in the industry.

Almost as striking as the information-organizing effectiveness of the market system is its stimulation of the participants toward a special type of behavior. Each decision unit is encouraged to act through the market in its own best interest.

Incentives and the Market System

The element both of carrot and stick is strong. For businessmen in a competitive environment the rule is: Be efficient or perish! Efficiency means higher profits, inefficiency means, in the long run, bankruptcy. Consumers may usually have more leeway but the punishment for erroneous decisions tends to come swiftly and to be recognized as such. The fact that the market separates out functional shares makes it much easier for an individual to identify the reason for success or failure. Thus the market serves to stimulate the narrowing of attention to those aspects of behavior that are most relevant for satisfaction maximizing by the household decision unit.

However, this very pattern of incentives which under competitive conditions tends to promote economic efficiency and even Pareto optimality has been the subject of a great deal of criticism. First there are the claims that it tends to select the wrong people as successes. Those who serve their own interests rather than those of society, those who are self-centered, and those who calculate in dollars and cents rather than in human values—these are the ones who are likely to come off best in a market environment. Thorstein Veblen suggested that a fundamental aspect of human motivation, the instinct for workmanship, tended to be perverted by the market place into a narrow commercial spirit which ignored quality and the pleasure of creating things. Others have tended to make a virtue of the skills of the market place, suggesting that it is a breeding ground of free men. In their view it is the independent, inner directed, self-starting and self-driving individual which the market system develops. Marketplace competition, it is claimed, cannot produce slaves since one can always quit one's job, change one's line of business. Violence is minimized by the rule of voluntary agreement so an attitude unfavorable to military adventurism tends to pervade the marketeers.

This question of the impact of the market system on the nature of man is one of the fundamental problems of human social organization. However, it deals primarily with issues which we cannot take up here. For an understanding of the manner in which the price system does its job it is more relevant for us to consider some of the ways in which the incentive system may fail to produce efficient outcomes. By now these will be familiar since they are associated with failings which have been discussed in previous sections. One important class of failings is associated with market structure. The monopolist not only is stimulated by the market to produce the wrong bill of goods. He may also fail to be stimulated to produce even those efficiently. The market gives the strongest push to those engaged in the keenest competition. A successful monopolist facing no immediate threat of entry may find it convenient to relax a bit and let others do the work even though they will do it less effectively. The "quiet life" incentive, as it has been called, may promote considerable inefficiency in concentrated markets. Much the same result may occur in a firm whose manager is not subject to close owner control.

Another incentive failure can grow out of external effects in the economy. When costs, like smog, are spread widely over a large number of people, no one person may be sufficiently harmed to have the incentive to try to protect himself against it. Nor does the smog producer have the incentive since it is far too costly to attempt to bargain with the victims for a smog-control subsidy. Only if some other incentive than narrow self-interest motivates a decision unit will smog control become a fact under these circumstances.

Another and possibly quite fundamental incentive failure occurs whenever there is a strong bargaining element in an economic situation. In this case the market creates the incentive to distort information as we have seen. It is difficult to determine how much distortion occurs and how long it can persist in the—informationally speaking—relatively open environment of a market economy. But pervasive misinformation is quite possible. One important case may occur with respect to consumer-product information. A consumer with his limited information-processing capacity must rely on relatively simple rules to guide most of his budget decisions. He has not the resources to become informed in detail. At the same time he typically makes a quite wide variety of purchases, involving hundreds of different items per year, even if he is very poor. This opens up real opportunities for misleading. The size and shape of containers may mislead as to contents. Advertising may suggest characteristics that are not present in the good or serve to suggest that more is there than an informed consumer would believe. Fears and hopes can be played on to stimulate purchases that would not have occurred with the well-informed consumer. A consumer with access to no information but that provided in advertising may persist for years in purchases that an hour of education as to the properties of alternatives would change.

Note that there are two sources of market failure involved in the above. The first is the element of bargaining. By advertising, the producer-distributor is entering into preliminary bargaining for a series of deals with perhaps millions of consumers, more or less simultaneously. At the same time he may have some competitors who are doing the same. Even though there is no personal contact between consumer and producer, the course of an advertising campaign has certain features in common with ordinary face-to-face negotiations for a deal. Through bargaining the market creates one type of incentive to misallocate resources.

The second element of failure comes from the consumer himself. The problem of consumer inefficiency, even given that he possesses accurate information, may be quite a serious one. For it is very costly to process the information sufficiently to know what characteristics each product possesses and then to determine which bundle of products provides the most efficient bundle of characteristics. This is a failure of consumer-processing capacity and is not attributable to misleading advertising. In part it is an external effect, a state that might be improved by collective generation of efficient decision rules for consumers. In part also it is simply a technical property of the environment and thus incorrigible so long as the existing human material participates in the economy.

A final instance of the incentive-pattern failure of a market system has to do with the dynamics of the adjustment process. One of the more exotic denizens of the market environment is the speculator. In effect he is a kind of assistant market organizer. His economic function is to speed the process of establishing equilibrium prices. The speculator sees his chance to make a profit when market prices differ from equilibrium prices. For example if there are several different price offers in a given market the speculator will buy the goods offered at the lower price and sell them at the higher price. This reduces the offers at both above- and below-equilibrium prices. Speculators have an incentive to continue the operation until there are no more such deals available. They police markets to ensure that only equilibrium prices are offered.

This is a rather striking instance of the ways in which the market system creates incentives to improve the operation of the system. However, this incentive, too, can break down and lead to unstable rather than stable outcomes. One possibility is that speculators conspire to create false impressions. In this way they may encourage the outsiders' false impression as to the equilibrium price level and then use their inside knowledge of the true level to profit on the return to equilibrium. Another possibility, which reflects less credit on the speculator's skills, is that he, too, is sometimes mistaken as to the equilibrium price and promotes inefficient allocations as a result. In current markets this is less likely to happen, since the corrective forces are there in the form of current supply and demand. But in markets where the future is essentially involved, as in many capital markets and markets for future goods, the speculator's swiftly changing expectations of the future state of the market can at times have a profoundly disruptive effect.

The Market and Creativity

One of the more fundamental aspects of the market economy has as yet never been captured in a formal model of the economy. This may be called its creativity, its tendency to produce change. This tendency in turn is a product of the informational openness of the system and its incentive patterns. The very nature of the market system ensures that a great deal of information is readily available to any participant. This is particularly true with respect to prices and to at least some of the characteristics of goods. But also there is a great deal of information publicly available about opportunities in the form of the profitabilities of various lines of activity. Typically, some expenditure of resources is necessary before an economically meaningful assessment of opportunities can be generated; and often this expenditure is fairly substantial and even then somewhat uncertain. But the amount of basic information available to the searcher is very great and is already partly organized in economically useful ways.

Combined with this is the incentive system, which provides financial rewards to the successful realizer of these opportunities. But the incentive system does more than this: it also gives considerable stimulus to some participants to assist others in realizing opportunities. The firm which hopes to find new markets for its products as inputs of a new enterprise or industry is an instance of this supporting incentive. This kind of stimulus is largely a consequence of the system of reward in terms of functional shares. When each factor is, as a consequence of the market process, rewarded in terms of the money measure of its contribution, it becomes relatively easier to put together new packages of factors in order to realize opportunities. Thus the information, incentive, and reward structure of the market system combine to provide a powerful stimulus to creativity.

Of course this aspect, too, of the market system is far from flawless. The distortions of efficiency that can occur in the market are also capable of distorting and suppressing creativity. A monopolist may sit on a new invention because it would reduce his profits, though a more competitive market structure would adopt the innovation. A competitive industry, its participants concerned with survival in the shorter run, may have no time left over to search widely for those innovations with more distant prospects of paying out. Enterprises may be reluctant to reveal the sources of internal improvements in efficiency which could improve the effectiveness of competitors. Uncertainty and risk aversion stemming from imperfections in the adjustment structure of markets reduce the expectation of profits from ventures below the socially desirable level; or, as with the small businesses already mentioned, excessive optimism produces the opposite effect of too many highly risky ventures. And so forth through the whole gamut of failures of the market system. Nevertheless this creative aspect of the market economy can easily be underestimated by those whose attention is too narrowly concentrated on models of efficient allocation with respect to the existing stock of resources and techniques.

Another and somewhat more speculative aspect of the market economy is perhaps also worth a few words. This is the creative response of the system itself, its tendency to generate internally corrections of its failures. This is a property that some social organisms possess. For example, if a colony of bees is stripped of the age group of bees who secrete the wax needed in cell construction, the older and the younger bees begin to produce again or prematurely these secretions, thus correcting automatically a possibly fatal blow to the social organism. To what extent does the market system possess this self-repairing feature?

A group of nineteenth-century economists known as the Social

Darwinists were optimistic on this score. It was their belief that the market tended to be wholly self-repairing. Thus the riskiness of capital ventures in competitive markets was thought to preclude the development of excessive concentrations of wealth which might seriously reduce the effectiveness of markets via powerful monopoly concentrations. "Shirtsleeves to shirtsleeves in three generations" was the slogan for this point of view. But this seems too sanguine a view, especially since the risk of ruin tends to decline with the relative size of enterprise, and wealth also is related to political power, so that the wealthy may help propagate their condition by promoting legislation favoring the wealthy.

Nevertheless the market system does possess some self-correcting mechanisms, at least under certain circumstances. The creativity discussed above is an important example of this. One of the reasons that monopoly has proved to be a less serious threat than it otherwise would be is the existence of market forces stimulating the development of new products. The existence of a monopoly with its high profit levels promotes the search for close substitutes for the monopolized goods. Even if they are far from perfect substitutes, they offer the prospect of draining off some of the monopoly profits into other hands. The mere threat of this affects the behavior of the monopolist himself, tending perhaps to reduce the price he charges to a lower level. Of course the monopolist, too, may search for such products and the outcome is by no means certain.

Another area of self-correcting lies in the use of misleading information. The very openness of the market economy reduces the extent to which, in the long run, such distributions may persist. Thus the economic reformer may find profit in providing reliable market information—at a price. Or he may see his opportunity in producing —and advertising—a good which provides characteristics more efficiently to the consumer than existing commodities.

Changes in market economies over the last century have been so great that it is virtually impossible to evaluate the extent to which these forces operate and, in particular, to evaluate their power to correct inefficiencies in the environments to be expected in the coming decades. It is certainly possible to conceive of environments in which the market mechanism would not work well at all. If, for example, automation were to produce a high level of interaction in production among existing enterprises, so that nonmarket interactions among firms were necessary to an ever-increasing extent in order to realize production efficiencies, the market would lose much of its ability both to signal efficient production and to allocate resources efficiently among competing uses. Economies of scale extending over the relevant range of demand throughout the economy, and externalities of the same magnitude could each destroy the market mechanism as an efficient allocator of resources. At the moment economists as a group have no clear expectations as to the direction of long-term trends in the economy. The recent past does suggest, however, that market growth and creativity have, on the whole, served fairly well to compensate tendencies toward inefficiency.

11

Government and the
Market Economy

The preceding chapter summarized some of the good and bad things about the ways in which market economies can work. However, nowhere was there any explicit mention of the role that government could or should play in such economies. It is time now to take some account of the behavior of this third broad class of decision makers.

Let us start with an idealized account of the government's role, one which assigns it the task of making the market system produce optimal results. Such a government—we will ignore the possibility of multiple governments making decisions in the same economy—must first form an opinion as to what is best for society so as to have a basis for evaluating alternatives. This is sometimes called a social-welfare function and serves precisely the same function for our government as profit maximization does for an enterprise and satisfaction maximization for a household. However, we do not inquire at the moment just what this social welfare is, and simply assume that the government knows what it is and tries to maximize it.

The next step is for the government to consider the various means by which it can influence the economy. These are sometimes called *instruments* and consist of such things as taxes of various kinds and amounts, price controls, regulations, and so forth. The government must know what the impact of each of these will be on economic outcomes—that is, it must know how each household and enterprise is affected if an instrument is applied to the economy. This knowledge provides the government with information about feasible alternatives, that is, about alternatives that it can bring to reality by using various combinations of instruments and of intensities of application of those instruments.

Now the government is ready to make its decision as to how to behave. It values each of these feasible alternatives in terms of the social-welfare function and chooses that alternative, that pattern of instruments, which provides the highest level of social welfare. The grand interaction of government, business, and households now produces a result which corrects the defects described in Chapter 10 and creates the best of all possible economic outcomes.

Unfortunately this is a poor description of how any real government has actually behaved. In the first place, governments rarely have a set of goals that are sufficiently clear and precise to make possible consistent judgments among policies in the way suggested. In a democratic society a variety of pressures from interest groups, some representing various interpretations of the public interest, some representing their own interest, are brought to bear during the governmental decision process. The result is likely to reflect the political conflict and balance of power among these interests rather than the maximum value of some a priori criterion.

In the second place, even if there were such a criterion, economists could not provide the required description of policies and their effects. We are still quite ignorant as to the consequences of many of the policies actually used by governments. Economists disagree as to the magnitude of their impact and sometimes even as to the direction of impact.

Nevertheless a more modern version of this idealized description does have its place in governmental decision making about economic matters. Its place comes early in the decision process and is generally limited to problems of relatively narrow scope. And it is provided, by and large, by economists. This is the stage of technical exploration of alternatives in which some kinds of economic analysis can be brought to bear on problems so as to clarify some properties of alternatives. The aim is not so much to make decisions as to prepare the ground for decision making by displaying possibly desirable alternatives and their properties. Also the clearly undesirable alternatives can be eliminated at this early stage, thus making the work of the political decision makers that much easier. Programming or systems analysis, as this approach is called, has been widely applied within the government of the United States in recent years, most especially in the Department of Defense.

In the sections that follow we will look at the problem areas of the market economy as described in the last chapter and consider a few of the instruments that have been used by governments in an attempt to improve on market outcomes. Our aim is twofold: first to show how price theory can be useful in the evaluation of alternatives open to government, and second to survey the more important areas in which government policy has had a significant impact on the economy. Because the means and ends of government are not so sharply separated as our idealization suggested, and because many instruments have an impact in more than one problem area, it is not always easy to classify an instrument with respect to the problem area. So our classification is rather arbitrary and is aimed at problems rather than instruments.

Equilibrium and Policy Instruments

In a sense nearly all government instruments are designed to alter the equilibrium position of an economy. This is true more or less by definition, since economists almost always work with models in which the properties of the equilibrium are of central interest. In this section we will be concerned with problems that can be usefully treated within the framework of equilibrium shifts using the traditional static analysis, and in particular with instruments which require direct control of market price or output.

Public Utility Pricing

An aspect of the monopoly problem illustrates the use of price theory in evaluating government policy alternatives. Suppose there is an industry, perhaps a public utility such as a local gas works or a hydroelectric project, which has strongly decreasing average cost as described in Figure 11.1. Given the demand curve, it is clear that only a single firm can survive in this industry. If left alone a profit-maximizing firm will adopt the usual monopolist's price and output policy, represented by point M on the diagram. The question before the government is whether to regulate the industry by controlling price or to live with the monopoly; additionally, if the government decides to regulate the industry, what price should it charge?

Let us first consider the question of what price to charge, given that the decision is to regulate the industry, and then compare our answer with the unregulated monopoly outcome. Price theory has told us that in a competitive economy the appropriate price is equal to marginal cost. If this price p_c is simply imposed on the industry there will be no output at all in the long run, for the enterprise would operate at a loss and investors would stay away. So either the price

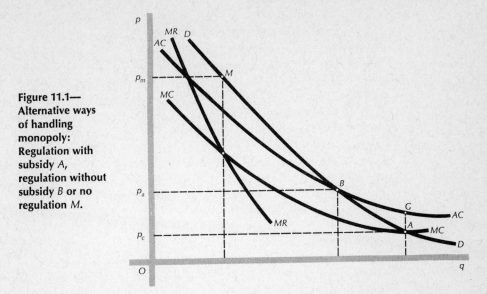

**Figure 11.1—
Alternative ways
of handling
monopoly:
Regulation with
subsidy A,
regulation without
subsidy B or no
regulation M.**

must be set at least at p_a, where demand and average-total-cost curves intersect, or the difference between average cost and p_c per unit must be given the enterprise as a subsidy. Which of these alternatives is preferable is a matter of dispute among economists; the solution to the question depends on a general equilibrium analysis which includes consideration of the consequences of the government paying a subsidy—that is, the government must obtain the resources to subsidize the industry from somewhere, so the value of alternative uses of the resources when p_c is chosen must be weighed against the distorting effects of a nonefficiency price p_a. Let us assume that the decision turns out to be in favor of p_a and no subsidy. If the industry is to be regulated, p_a will be the regulated price.

Now the outcomes represented by points M and A must be compared. A major conclusion that emerges from a look at the diagram would be the following:

▶▶   *Ceteris paribus, the less elastic the demand for the product
between A and M the stronger the case for regulation.*

For, other things being equal, the steeper the demand curve, the greater the monopoly price differential and the smaller the relative output of the monopolist. It takes resources to regulate an industry. Also there is an information problem, as the enterprise has an incentive to exaggerate its costs, shifting up its apparent average cost curve so as to get a higher price from the regulatory commission. If there are fairly close substitutes for the product of the industry, the gain from regulation may not be worth the cost of regulation.

Naturally this highly simplified analysis is insufficient to produce a good practical decision. What we have done is apply a partial analysis of some important factors relevant to the decision. A good deal of work remains before a final decision can be made. Other alternatives, such as nationalization, may be considered. And other aspects of the problem must be carefully considered. For example, a demand curve based on historical data may not take account of the possible entry of new firms to the region if the price of a basic input such as power is cheaper here than in other regions. A monopolist may not have the incentive to seek out new techniques and new uses of the product so as to stimulate such entry. On the other side of the ledger, government regulation of the industry may divert energies from such considerations of competition, or may create uncertainties in the minds of potential new entrants as to future industry policy by making the industry a political football. And if other prices are not competitive, there is less presumption of inefficiency in a monopoly price for this industry. Price theory can provide some narrowing of the range of possible outcomes, but cannot confidently evaluate all the consequences of the decision.

Farm Income Supports

Another application of price theory is in the evaluation of the cost to government of alternative schemes to support farm incomes. Suppose the government is committed to providing the farmers as a group with given income. The income is determined by some formula relating present and past farm incomes, or perhaps relating current farm income to current incomes in other lines of work. Suppose this commitment to maintain a predetermined farm income level has already been made. On our supply and demand diagrams this can be represented by an area, since price times quantity equals revenue. The government is considering three alternative instruments: (1) to set a minimum price at which it is prepared to buy any amount of domestic production offered to it; (2) to let farm prices find their equilibrium on the market and provide a direct grant to farmers to make up any deficit with respect to the targeted income; and (3) to control production directly so as to get the equilibrium supply of the farm products, paying farmers a price for this which gives them the targeted income and then reselling the crop on the market at the lower equilibrium price. Which of these alternatives should the government choose?

The problem is illustrated for a product in inelastic demand in Figure 11.2a. D is the demand curve, S the supply curve. OEFG shows farm revenue under market conditions, in which F is the

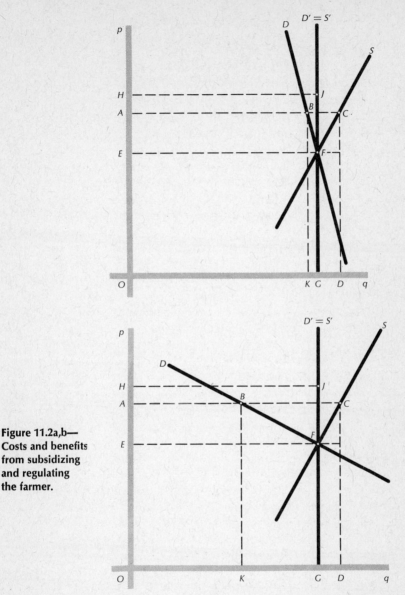

**Figure 11.2a,b—
Costs and benefits
from subsidizing
and regulating
the farmer.**

equilibrium point; however, targeted farm income is the larger
amount represented by area *OACD*. If the first alternative is chosen,
the government will set minimum price at *OA*. At this price the
private sector of the economy will take *AB* of the product and the
excess supply, *BC*, will be bought by the government at the support
price. Farmers get the targeted income and the government must

159

pay *KBCD* in order to sustain the policy, getting in return *BC* of the crop which it cannot resell on the domestic market without torpedoing its policy.

With the second policy farmers produce and sell on the private market *EF* of the crop. However, the government must provide them with supplemental income represented by the area *EHJF*. This is clearly greater than *KBCD*, so this policy is more costly in terms of direct support to farmers. The third policy has the government directly controlling the amount produced by each farmer, buying the crop at a price *OH* which produces the targeted income (the figure is drawn so that the two areas, *OHJG* and *OACD*, are equal) and reselling on the private market at the equilibrium price. The cost to the government is again *EHJF*, so here again the price-support policy is cheaper.

However, if product demand is relatively elastic the relative cost is reversed, as is shown in Figure 11.2b. Again the second and third policies are tied in terms of support cost to the government, but each is less costly than the price-support program. This suggests that a support program, given that one of these three policies must be adopted, might take a different form with different crops, depending on product demand elasticity. Again, this deals with only part of the problem. The administrative costs and effectiveness of alternate control schemes vary widely. For example, it is likely to be easier to control the price of the product than its output. The former requires the setting of only a single magnitude for each product and the policing of markets is relatively simple, since the government is prepared to buy any amount at the given price. Output control, however, requires some regulation of perhaps hundreds of thousands of magnitudes, representing the output of the product by every actual or potential producer.

And of course in the case of price supports the government receives a portion of the crop. If it can find some use for the crop, for example as an adjunct to the foreign aid program or as a domestic hedge against poor crop years, this gain must be added to the opportunity cost of the price support policy. On the other hand, the high support price is inefficient if markets are competitive and so implies a direct malallocation of resources. Also the artificially high price should serve to encourage more investment in the "industry" producing that crop than would otherwise occur, thus shifting the supply curve out and making the long-run costs to the price-support program tend to increase. Finally, the different schemes have different consequences for income distribution among farmers. A price-support program provides more income to large producers than to small, though the aim of the program is presumably to aid the small producers. All these factors should be taken into account before a final decision is made.

Excise vs. Income Tax

A final example of direct allocative intervention in markets by government is that of choosing between an excise tax and an income tax. The former is a tax per unit on the production or sale of a good, the latter an across-the-board tax on each household. Suppose for the moment that all individuals have the same income and the same

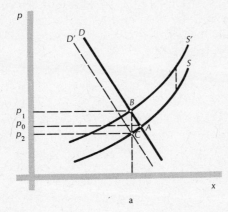

Figure 11.3a—The price effect of this excise tax is borne mainly by consumers; that is, $(p_1 - p_0)$ is greater than $(p_0 - p_2)$.

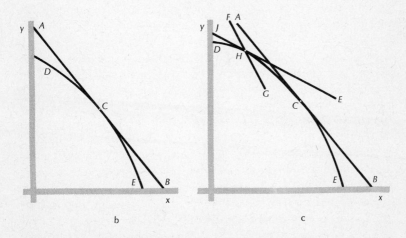

Figure 11.3b,c—If producers receive a different price than consumers pay, allocative efficiency is affected.

attitude toward the two goods produced by the private sector of an economy. Suppose also that the government has already decided to obtain a given amount of resources for its programs and that the only question at issue is whether to raise the necessary resources by an income or an excise tax. Let us also suppose that the private sector of the economy is competitive.

Figure 11.3a shows the impact of an excise tax on industry X. Before the tax the industry was in equilibrium at A. The effect of the tax is to raise the marginal cost at every level of output by the amount of the tax, assuming the firms in the industry pay the tax to the government. This is quivalent to an upward shift of the supply curve at every level of output by the amount of the tax (why?). Consequently the new equilibrium is at B and the price is p_1. The effect has been to raise equilibrium price substantially. Indeed the consumer has absorbed most of the price rise. On the other hand, there has been a relatively small reduction in output. The reason is again the elasticity of demand. For a more elastic product demand the industry would absorb a larger part of the tax and there would be a relatively greater effect on output.

For our decision the important thing to note is that the effective price to consumers is now different than that to producers. The price to consumers is now p_1. However, the price that is of interest to producers is that net of the tax, or p_2. This can be seen by noting that our result is not changed if it is the consumers rather than the producers who pay the tax to government. Then the demand curve becomes in effect D', which is shifted down from D by the same amount as S' was shifted up from S, reflecting the fact that the consumers now demand an amount determined by B, the tax rate plus the market price. Clearly this curve intersects S directly below point B.

Now turn to Figure 11.3b where both goods that are privately produced in our simple economy are depicted and the production possibilities represented by curve DCE. If the economy were in equilibrium with a proportional deduction from all incomes as a result of an income tax, the price ratios between producers and consumers would not be changed at all, so the income tax equilibrium would be represented by a point like C. ACB is the price line for this equilibrium. Consumers get maximum satisfaction at C. They would not choose any other feasible point since its money value would be less than that at C.

However, the effect of an excise tax would be to cause consumers to choose a point other than C. The price ratios between consumers and producers are no longer the same as a result of this tax. Since the economy remains competitive, producers will move out to the production frontier and their effective equilibrium price ratio will be tangent to *DE*, for example at *H* in Figure 11.3c. However, the consumer price ratio is different; it might be *FG* in Figure 11.3c, assuming the tax is levied on *X*, making its relative price to consumers higher than to producers. Consumers would prefer *C* if they had the choice, but the price system no longer gives them that choice as a result of the distorted price ratios. So our conclusion is that the income tax is preferred to the excise tax as a revenue instrument, other things equal.

Again, of course, this is not a sufficient basis for making a final judgment on these two taxes. First it should be noted that we assumed competitive conditions. If they are absent then our conclusion does not follow. Indeed it might even be reversed. Suppose, for example, that the economy was initially at point *H* of Figure 11.3c as a result of market imperfections. Now a wisely chosen excise tax might move it back to *C*, whereas an income tax would make things still worse. Also we have ignored effects on income distribution. We assumed equality among individuals so as to be able to say that what happened on the average, as depicted by the maximum satisfaction points for total output of the product in the diagrams, also applied to each individual. But in practice incomes diverge widely and taxes have redistributive effects. An excise on an item consumed only by the well-to-do—large yachts, Russian caviar—may have only a trivial effect on resource allocation and also move income distribution in a desired direction. Also, in practice, income taxes do tend to have some excise effects, for example, because income does not include the value of leisure. Thus we have only provided one piece in the policy puzzle as a consequence of our analysis in terms of elementary price theory.

By and large governments have not taken a fundamental interest **Adjustment** in the adjustment process in individual markets. Of course the question of over-all stability, the basic problem of macroeconomics, is a central concern of governments in market economies because of the widespread desire to maintain high employment levels. However, academic division of labor leads us to ignore this problem right now. It is true that single-market adjustment problems have been given limited attention by governments; it is probably also true that inerest in developing instruments of policy in this area is increasing.

Adjustment can fail if expectations become destabilizing, if technical time lags in adjustment are very long, or if lags caused by deficiencies in economic organization occur. The natural instruments for dealing with these phenomena entail either adjusting the timing of the lags or adjusting the amplitude of response.

Government control of the stock market and of some commodity markets illustrates the attempt to control response amplitude. The

Federal Reserve Board, for example, has the power to set and vary margin requirements, that is to fix the maximum proportion of the value of a stock an investor can borrow from brokers in order to purchase the stock. This gives the Board the power to make a given amount of money more or less powerful in bidding up the value of a stock. If speculators appear to be entering the market in large numbers, they will in all likelihood be buying on margin. By raising the margin requirements the speculation becomes relatively less attractive and so a speculation-induced "bubble" of deviation of stock prices from their current equilibrium can be dampened.

For some years American governments have intervened to speed up the adjustment process in the labor maarket. The principal instrument for this purpose is labor exchanges. Offices are set up in major cities and around farm areas where there is a seasonal demand for labor. These offices collect information about job and personnel availability, provide office space for interviewing, and generally support the market process of making deals for units of this imperfectly substitutable commodity. As a consequence of improving the organization of the market, deals should generally tend to be closer to the equilibrium price, and with the information better organized the average length of time needed to make a deal should be reduced.

As a final aspect of adjustment it might be well to mention the relation between population growth and growth of the labor force. There appears to be a connection between the birth rate and general economic conditions, so that, other things equal, in relatively prosperous years more children will be born than in years of recession or depression. The additional children, in part a response to good times, become additions to the labor force about eighteen years later. There is virtually no connection between economic conditions in one year and those eighteen years later. Consequently this fairly rigid time lag creates special problems of economic adjustment, and there seems to be little likelihood that the problem can be dealt with by operating on the early end of the process. In the United States the baby boom after World War II has produced studies, both government-sponsored and private, of the ways in which labor supply would be affected. Anticipatory building of schools in advance of the bulge did occur. Perhaps the large-scale labor force entry of recent years has had some impact on various aspects of the War on Poverty. However, it is not clear that any direct instruments for adjusting specifically to the baby boom have been developed.

Information   The control and manipulation of information flows has been one of the major occupations of modern governments, democratic and totalitarian alike. In the more democratic states of course the control has been much less systematic and less oriented toward the restriction of political information flows. But the substantial nature of controls, even in democratic societies, is easily documented.

Quite a variety of information-control instruments have been employed by the United States government. Some are the result of technical conditions. FCC regulation of television licensing is a response to the externalities of communication: one station alone can broadcast on a particular channel, there are a limited number of channels (at least in the normal frequency range) and so the opportunities for technical monopoly are rather good. Many have argued that there are externalities of consumption with respect to television broadcasts, which prevent the market mechanism from producing efficient outcomes. The argument is essentially that there are economies of scale with respect to consumption of television programs which lead networks and advertisers to choose only programs that will have a wide appeal. The consumer's alternative of switching channels or turning off the set is not a budget allocation device, so that the intensity of small-scale program preference cannot be effectively signaled to the producers. A second argument relating to consumption externalities is that consumers choose unwisely; that is that they tend to prefer vulgar entertainment to the near exclusion of other types of programs which in some sense they should consume, at least part of the time.

One response to this has been for the FCC to attempt to influence programming, using as its instrument its power to refuse to grant or renew licenses and its own access to information media. Another has been to encourage the establishment of noncommercial television stations in a number of cities. Such stations are partly subsidized and, in few cases, are based on listener sponsorship via contributions. In the latter case the "volunteer fire department" problem arises that it is in each listener's material interest to encourage others to subscribe but not to do so himself. As always with information questions it is very difficult to evaluate alternative proposals because of the inability of the market to place an efficiency price on alternative types of communications.

Another and probably more important type of government involvement in information is the broad-scale collection and processing of information about the performance of the economy. The Statistical Abstract of the United States provides a general collection of statistics about recent performance of a great many sectors of the economy, including price and output data, information on population structure, investment, incomes, and so forth. Behind this collection, which in a typical year contains over 100,000 items of information, lies a vast series of collection services, only a tiny fraction of whose product resides in the Abstract. This effort may be viewed as an instrument whose function is to identify failings in the market economy and to evaluate the performance of policies. A considerable fraction of the information, even though it has no national security relevance, is not available to the public.

The government has also developed information processing services for private decision units. This can, for example, reduce the impact of inefficiency in consumption patterns in cases in which the processing of technical information needed to determine the characteristics of products is beyond the capacity of ordinary consumers. One of the first interventions of this kind in the United States was the Pure Food and Drug Act which, in its present form, sets a variety of restrictions on the way in which many drug products are described and labeled. Under present (1966) discussion is a bill which would control the packaging and size and weight labeling of many foodstuffs. Research into the efficiency of consumer choice has hardly begun, but would seem to be out of direct relevance in evaluating the net benefits to be derived from legislation of this kind.

This sort of information control by government may also be used as an instrument for controlling the bargaining process. The incentive to mislead in bargaining over a deal has already been discussed. One way for a powerful potential seller to bargain for a higher than equilibrium price is to increase the costs to the opposite party of finding out the true characteristics of his good. Even with a high-level information-processing capacity the potential buyer may be induced to accept a higher price so long as the costs of processing are significant. Regulation of advertising by the FCC as well as truth-in-packaging legislation and purely informational services may be effective instruments, one of whose consequences is a speeding up of the adjustment process and a diminution in the range of prices that persists around equilibrium.

Finally the government is involved in a major effort to support research and development or the creation of new information. This can serve as an instrument to improve the private market equilibrium. Since the profits from new information generation are often not capturable, or only partly capturable by the creator, the market mechanism may fail to stimulate a number of worthy investigations.

A second argument is that research expenditures are an instrument for the correction of the private-market interest rate. It has been argued that this rate is higher than that required to generate a Pareto optimum. Partly this is because consumers, acting in the market place in a series of individual decisions, have little or no incentive to take into account long-run considerations, such as the kind of economy they will turn over to the next generation. Only in political decision making is this longer-range question considered.

Since most people, it is argued, are willing to make some present sacrifices in order to leave a good plant as a legacy for the unborn, and since the market rate does not reflect this preference, the resulting equilibrium interest rate is too high. The subsidizing of reseach is one device by which the government can give some direct stimulus to the adoption by decision units of longer time horizons than are generated by the market. Another argument along these lines is that the market breaks up risk and tends to make situations in which individual decision units operate riskier than those in which society as a whole functions. The individual only survives in the short run while society is expected to survive in the long run. However, it is not at all clear how different kinds of risk at government and private decision levels will affect attitudes toward the future. For example, the bureaucratic organization of government may make it a strong risk averter and may make officials very shortsighted, concerned only with the state of affairs during their brief tenure in a specific position.

Research subsidies, however, introduce another important consideration. In fact the government has become a major supporter of research primarily in connection with the military and space programs. These programs have a special property, namely that there is a strong interdependence in production between the private and public sectors. The government cannot leave product development to private industry and simply send buyers out to look around in tank-producers' showrooms until they find a model that best suits the military's needs. A major reason for this is that the government's final product, the capability to carry out certain military missions, has many properties which are not public knowledge, and which cannot be made public. The military establishment is in a position to determine what it would like its equipment to do, but it is largely in the private production establishment that what in fact can be done is determined. This situation requires a great deal of nonmarket negotiation and actual supervision of parts of the production process by the government. And nowhere is the need for government involvement greater than in the development of new weapons and the development of the capability to develop new weapons. It is the latter aspect of the government's involvement that has led to much sponsorship of research, for the development of knowledge necessary for the creation of weapon systems of the more distant future is a concern that devolves more on government than on a private concern, which cannot easily anticipate whether the new knowledge will be of benefit to its own production capabilities.

Information and incentives are very closely connected, as the last example or two of the preceding section have shown. However, some

Incentives

aspects of incentives are of quite direct concern to government, and some instruments seem clearly aimed at altering the incentive pattern. In a sense these are the most fundamental interventions in the market mechanism which governments may undertake.

One of the major problems that a government engaged in large-scale diversion of resources from the market faces is how to divert the resources with minimal disturbance of the market process and particularly of the incentives normally generated in the market. An example or two of the price and output effects of government resource diversion have already been discussed. We will not go into this further except to note that it often requires difficult decisions of a "second best" nature. That is, either the market is not in competitive equilibrium or government actions are such—perhaps on such a large scale—that market measures of the effects on the private sector are in neither case an accurate measure of social effects. This puts the government in the position of comparing two outcomes neither of which is efficient. Unfortunately price theory does not as yet give much help in resolving such questions.

On the incentive side, however, there is one device which is widely used which make use of the economist's concept of margins. This is the marginal tax rate, which operates to provide some continuing private incentive to increase income while siphoning large fractions of consumer income to the government budget. Thus an individual in the highest income tax bracket may have seventy cents out of each additional dollar of income diverted to the government. Nevertheless he still retains thirty cents on each additional dollar earned, and this provides him with at least some material incentive to continue to increase his income. The same approach has been suggested as a subsidizing device for the poor in the form of a negative income tax. Thus, for example, a family earning $2,000 a year might be eligible for a $1,000 subsidy. If the family has an opportunity to increase its income by a hundred dollars, the subsidy may fall by, say, only fifty dollars. Consequently, by taking the opportunity family income goes up to $2,050, thus providing a continual marginal incentive to increase privately earned income.

The government does not follow this policy everywhere, however. For example, social security and unemployment benefits are paid in such a way as to discourage the recipient from increasing his privately earned income above a certain amount. In this case government operation in the market place does substantially distort individual incentives.

Another and more fundamental government expenditure which has impact on incentives is education. Part of a citizen's education gives him a greater capacity to process market information and an expanded capacity to acquire certain kinds of skills that may be valued on the market. Expectation that one might succeed in performing valuable activities is an important element in the incentive to try, so in this sense education does affect incentives strongly. In addition, of course, it serves to expand the range of skills that the market may successfully call forth, to reduce the length of time that many kinds of adjustment in the employed worker skill mix would take and to substitute for the market in providing knowledge and skills that the market would provide if the government did not. In addition, education is to some extent a consumer good, a service which many will be willing to buy simply for the pleasure of consumption and regardless of the existence of any political or economic payoffs to the recipient. Separating these various aspects of education is no easy matter; it might be argued, however, that at least part of the latter two functions can be provided efficiently by the market mechanism, so that on efficiency grounds some of these kinds of educational services need not be provided by the government.

Contract Law

Long before governments were deeply involved in universal education of the citizenry they were deeply involved in controlling some of the properties of deals made on their territories. Much of this control is exercised through the law of contract and of torts. And much of this regulation seems to be clearly a matter of the exercise of coercion by government in the interest of increasing welfare, the material well-being of the populace. The first big step by governments was to force men, through the courts, to keep their promises with respect to a wide variety of deals. Later courts became prepared to support the sale of promises. The promises contained in negotiable instruments, or deals the cost and benefits from which could be sold to others, also became enforceable. More recently a number of restrictions on the terms of deals have developed within the American and other judicial systems.

The doctrine of product liability can serve to illustrate the motivation of these developments. An automobile owner who suffers an accident as the result of a defect in his machine may be able to recover damages from the manufacturer, even though it was a third party who sold him the car. The idea is that the manufacturer now has some responsibility to turn out a product with the characteristics a potential purchaser may reasonably expect it to have. Clearly this seems to be a judicial response—the doctrine has developed in the courts by decisions of judges at least as much as from direct legislation—to the greatly increased information-processing demand made on contemporary consumers. By changing the consumer's expectations as to the consequences of purchase, the courts in effect produce a consumer who, other things qeual, is more willing to buy than he would otherwise be. And the producer acquires by the judicial acts a stronger incentive to engage in careful quality control of his product. It may also affect his advertising, since by advertising the manufacturer may be able to influence the consumer's "reasonable expectations."

Why should the government create a body of law which forces people to keep their promises? Essentially this is the chief function that the earliest versions of the law of contract performed. They made it possible for an individual to obtain government assistance in penalizing a partner to a deal who did not perform according to the terms of the contract. For example, anyone who hopes to make a series of deals with individuals in contact with one another over a period of time has an incentive to perform, at least on the early contracts, in order to establish the expectation in the minds of those who may make later deals with him that he will perform. Clearly a good deal of trade could be carried out without a government-enforced law of contract. The answer seems clear: the government provides a contract-enforcing mechanism through the legal and judicial system in order to reduce the risks of contract making. This in turn serves to increase the number of deals that will be made. And we have seen that this creates some presumption of an increase in welfare, since the deals themselves are made voluntarily and so presuppose that each party expects to benefit as a result. The law of contract is a welfare-increasing government intervention in the market mechanism.

The extent to which contracts are regulated by government has increased in a great variety of ways in the last half-century. As an instrument for the protection of labor most employment contracts now require that certain terms be considered part of the contract, for example setting maximum hours of regular work. In the nineteenth century the United States outlawed slavery, which eliminated a whole class of contracts from private consideration. In the twentieth century it has forbidden a variety of contracts of employment of children. In many other areas, such as gambling, the sale of narcotics and many other kinds of drugs, the government has sharply restricted the range and terms of private contracts. Though little over-all planning goes into most of the developments in this area, it appears to be a very widely used government instrument for adjusting market equilibria.

Market Reorganization

A final class of government instruments contains the most spectacular ones in the government arsenal. These deal with the compulsory reorganization of markets. Major reorganizations raise fundamental political questions as to the admissible range of government instruments in a society which is committed to the preservation of the civil rights of the citizenry. However, for the moment let us ignore this issue and look very briefly at some of the instruments currently available to government in market economies and their economic implications.

Trust busting is such an instrument. An idealized version of this is to take a monopolized industry and through compulsory reorganization convert it into a competitive industry. If the monopolized industry has a number of plants, each of these may be converted into an independent enterprise and, provided conditions are compatible with the survival of competition, the newly formed industry may perform indefinitely to produce outcomes which, as we have seen, lead to more efficient outcomes in an otherwise competitive economy. Some students of American industry have felt that most structural imperfections are not the product of decreasing average cost situations, so that competition is a viable alternative to the present state of affairs. Obviously such a policy could be applied to concentrated oligopoly industries as well as to monopolies.

We have already seen some of the ways in which price theory can give insight into the effectiveness of such a policy instrument. Clearly it will fail if the conditions which led to concentration in the first place continue to operate. In this case the government must continue to intervene in the industry to prevent mergers or growth of individual firms to a point from which they can influence price by their own policies. Another issue has to do with the extent of admissible concentration in the industry. Here existing information does not provide a clear criterion, since, as we have seen, high profits are an ambiguous signal, possibly indicating effective management and technical progress rather than market imperfections.

Less drastic organizational measures are also available to the government, such as price regulation of utilities and the use of sanctions such as fines and prison sentences against businesses and businessmen who engage in acts asociated with monopolistic outcomes in a market. After the early days of the antitrust legislation, government action has been limited to these latter two types of action. They suffer from the disadvantage of being nonself-liquidating, since the control and supervision must be exercised continuously in contrast to once-and-for-all restructuring of the market. On the other hand they involve less drastic change and so are less destabilizing with respect to expectations.

A final dramatic form of market reorganization is nationalization of a firm or an industry. In the case of decreasing average cost industries, for example, this is a possible alternative to private monopoly or regulation of a private firm. Its advantage is that it eliminates the dual authority of operators and regulators of the second of our alternatives and, in principle at least, the incentive to produce non-optimal outcomes of the first alternative. However, the incentives the managers of the nationalized firm will bring to bear on their decision making are not very well understood. A variety of nationalized forms exist. Probably the most efficient is the public corporation in which the manager of the enterprise, though appointed by the government, has a considerable measure of autonomy with respect to government officials and legislators. He may bring some concept of the public interest to bear on his decision making, produce a price and output policy that takes some account of relevant nonmarket factors. He may also bring the bureaucrat's conservatism with him, leading to a technically stagnant and unprogressive pattern of decisions. Obviously such dramatic instruments have complex and not wholly certain consequences, a fact which may tend to inhibit their widespread use, at least in the United States.

Income Re-distribution In the idealized competitive model a legitimate role for government was recognized in redistributing wealth so that the market mechanism would produce an outcome that was both efficient and desirable on the distributive dimension. Nearly all government policy instruments have some redistributive effects, and many government instruments are applied with a view to deliberate redistribution.

On what grounds may one argue that one pattern of income is better than another? We will look briefly at four possible criteria for judging distributions.

The egalitarian position seems simple enough. Give everyone the same amount of money income. However, this would not be an egalitarian outcome in terms of several important aspects of the distribution. For example, it would mean that workers, like coal miners, performing hard, skilled labor, would receive the same income as those who performed sedentary, unskilled labor, like railroad-crossing tenders. Furthermore, the decision has to be made as to whether the distribution will be egalitarian with respect to families or individuals, and if the latter, whether children and old folks and women and the disabled should receive the same income as men. Then there is the question of ability and effort. One may still be an egalitarian and provide more for those who contribute more. And finally there is the question of differences in tastes. It may be that people differ so that an income that is quite satisfactory to one is viewed as a real hardship by another with different tastes. Only if all differences of this kind were to be ignored would an egalitarian want to equalize money incomes among families.

A second criterion is provided by some socialist thinkers. They would argue that some income is unearned and so, in a better organized society, would not be paid out. This is, roughly, income from property which, the Socialist would argue, is not a payment for any service performed by the recipient but is instead a surplus extracted from the rightful income of wage earners.

About one fourth of all personal income received in the United States is property income. As might be expected, most of this income is received by members of the top income groups, so that if they were not given the income the distribution would unquestionably be more equal. However, the dispersion of income would still be substantial. Tens of thousands of jobs pay upwards of $15,000 a year. On the other hand, the funds available from such a redistribution would certainly be enough substantially to reduce the poverty at the bottom end of the distribution.

This is a tenable moral position. There is no way to prove scientifically that it is wrong. However, that does not mean that one has to agree with it. One might argue that despite its form, property income *is* a reward for effort. Participants in a capitalist economy have the incentive to accumulate wealth so that they may pass on to their children (or to themselves in their old age) an income which is in effect a reward for past rather than present achievement. To argue that this is a good thing is also to argue from a tenable moral position with which one may agree or disagree depending on one's own moral values.

A third position might be that, though inequality is not only perfectly acceptable but even desirable in principle, in practice some people are paid too much and others too little. This is a very difficult position to evaluate, since our evaluations of the skills and efforts of others are likely to be strongly influenced by our own. One might argue, for example, that it is grossly unfair for farmers to be in a lower income bracket than unskilled city labor, since farming is a tough, skilled occupation. This argument has been made rather effectively by farmers themselves, and has been a factor in the government subsidizing of farm incomes.

The occurrence of sharp relative changes in incomes between occupations is a frequent basis for charges that incomes are unfair. For example, during the late 1930s and 1940s the incomes of doctors increased much faster than those of other professionals. This led to charges of unfair pricing, especially since part of the change was due to tight control of entry to the profession by the doctors' professional organization.

A final criterion is essentially a defense of the existing distributions. The argument is that in a market economy people earn what they get. For if they do not, who will hire them or buy their products? It is derived from marginal-productivity theory which says that in competitive equilibrium the wage of a worker is equal to the market value of his marginal product.[1] Since all factors are paid an amount equal to the market value of their marginal product, capitalists, too, are merely receiving "productivity payments" for the factors they own. What could be fairer than this? We have already noted that the competitive equilibrium may be consistent with great misery and that in imperfect markets factor prices may be greater or less than the market value of the marginal product. If it were true that over a broad range of redistributions of income, equilibrium-factor prices tended to change relatively little, then the argument that competitive market economies pay people what they are worth would be more plausible. However, if relative and absolute factor prices are strongly influenced by redistributions then it is hard to argue that people get what they are worth on markets without implicitly judging the income distribution itself as being optimal. Unfortunately we have little or no information on the empirical part of this question.

One more example of property rights giving advantages is a situation in which wealth gives political power. If the wealthy come to dominate the political process, they may pass laws favoring themselves and thus increase their income at the expense of the poorer classes, even though the market economy is preserved. Is this change in the income distribution deserved by both groups?

Naturally there is considerable disagreement as to which of these criteria is the appropriate one to apply. There is still another consideration, however, which has probably been of primary importance in stimulating redistributive policies. This is the widely recognized social goal of equalizing opportunity in the economy. Children in higher-income families have access to a wider range of processes which tend to improve their ability to operate on markets. The contrast is most striking between the literate and the illiterate, but the contrast does not stop there. In addition, the higher-income family is often more influential and so is able to obtain, within limits, preference for its children over other families. Finally the socializa-

1. The reader may remember the section on economic rent at this point and say: not so! All but the marginal unit of the factor receive more than is necessary to keep them in the present use whenever the supply curve for the factor is rising. Therefore when they were at the margin their marginal value productivity was less than at the given equilibrium. The defender of marginal productivity might reply: Suppose that, other things equal, one of those intramarginal units is removed from its present use; then the equilibrium-factor price does measure the value of the marginal product lost as a consequence.

tion process itself tends to promote and inhibit certain kinds of capabilities in children. For example, interest in professional careers is much more common among the children of middle-class families than among working-class children. Many programs of redistribution are therefore aimed at redressing the opportunity balance.

But opportunities are a rather vaguely defined concept. Many children of the disadvantaged poor are able to overcome their handicaps and achieve a larger measure of material success than many children of the well-to-do. It is the probability of achievement that is lower, not the certainty. A welfare program may then be interpreted as a kind of insurance scheme. For example, its purpose might be to provide a minimum expected value of achievement for every participant in the society. The expected value might be calculated as the expected income of each group having a given combination of the selected set of handicapping characteristics. This approach is roughly consistent with many of the existing welfare programs. However, it has the problems associated with all insurance schemes. In particular its effective administration calls for good information on the relevant probabilities and a pattern of benefits which does not distort normal market incentives. A somewhat deeper problem arises because of the tendency for social instruments to be blunt—that is, to affect more factors that the desired ones. For example, suppose the current pattern of tastes in society leads more children of a certain type of parent into occupation X, which is lower paid, than into occupation Y, and that this taste affects the probability of achievement. To what extent should the government attempt to alter the probability? In this case opportunities and tastes are closely intermingled. The welfare program designed to operate on this situation may be promoting conformity of attitude rather than equality of opportunity. The nature of instruments generally forces us to make hard decisions with respect to the appropriate mix of wanted and unwanted consequences of their application.

In considering some of the properties of market economies in this book we have, in different places, operated at different levels of abstraction. Our initial pieces of analysis assumed the world to be a very simple place: there was only one market capable of changing and the participants were concerned to make decisions in a certain world with respect to only one or two variables, such as price and output. Then we took some account of the effects of uncertainty and ignorance. Later we moved from partial to general equilibrium analysis in which account was taken of the mutual effects of changes in markets on one another. But still the analysis was couched in terms of a limited range of variables such as the amounts of goods produced or offered on markets and their prices. Finally in dealing

Economics and Society

175

with government we considered the use of some of the government's instruments for adjusting market outcomes with respect to a somewhat broader range of variables, including the pattern of income distribution among households and the effect of government instruments on the capacity of private decision units to process information. But even this is still partial analysis from the point of view of society. It should always be remembered that the economist deals with only a limited aspect of social reality while the economy has widespread impact on many other aspects of social behavior.

It is in this context that both the power and the limitations of price theory should be viewed. The behavioral scientist tends to look at society as an interacting collection of decision processes. The great power of economic theory stems from the fact that the market offers a device for measuring the value of alternatives to participants, so that many of their economic decision problems are much simpler than those relating to other kinds of social decisions. And behind this set of measurement devices, the equilibrium prices, lies the general equilibrium theory that tells us that under certain circumstances these prices may even provide moral measurements. That is, they may be used to measure the social value of various economic alternatives. There are no other social theories which are as powerful —which provide us with as much assistance in making decisions about as broad a range of problems as does price theory.

Nevertheless, as we have seen, existing market economies deviate significantly from the properties necessary to convert actual prices into moral measures. The extent of this deviation is problematical, the object of controversy on which reasonable men may differ. And even where the deviations are not deemed to be crippling, the issue remains as to whether a given alternative which passes the price-measurement test of optimality may be nonoptimal because of its political or sociological or psychological consequences. The student of price theory, even the student of market economies in general, can offer considerable assistance to others in clarifying their understanding of the alternatives before them. But judgment, common sense, and a recognition of the fact that economics is a form of partial analysis of social phenomena will remain as necessary ingredients of wise social decision making.

Additional Readings

Among the most useful of the more advanced treatments of the **More** **Advanced** theory of resource allocation are Milton Friedman, *Price Theory: A* **Texts** *Provisional Text* (Chicago: Aldine, 1962); and William Fellner, *Emergence and Contents of Modern Economic Analysis* (New York: McGraw-Hill, 1960). The former contains a systematic, technical treatment of topics while the latter emphasizes the origin and development of key ideas.

Several sides in the controversy over the appropriate economic **Government** role of government are presented in E. S. Phelps (ed.), *Private Wants* **and Market** *and Public Needs,* rev. ed. (New York: Norton [pb[1]], 1965). The libertarian and liberal positions are cogently presented in Milton Friedman, *Capitalism and Freedom* (Chicago: U. of Chicago Press [pb], 1962); and John Kenneth Galbraith, *The Affluent Society* (New York: Mentor [pb], 1958), respectively. For a stimulating theory of government decision making, see Anthony Downs, *An Economic Theory of Democracy* (New York: Harper, 1957).

Novel discussions of the role of information and uncertainty in **Consump-** consumption decisions can be found in Kelvin Lancaster, "Change **tion** and Innovation in the Technology of Consumption," *American Eco-*

1. Indicates availability of inexpensive paperback edition.

nomic Review (May 1966); George Katona, *The Mass-Consumption Society* (New York: McGraw-Hill, 1964); and David Caplovitz, *The Poor Pay More; Consumer Practices of Low-Income Families* (New York: Free Press, 1963). For empirical measurements of various consumption elasticities, see *A Study of Consumer Expenditures, Incomes and Savings* (Philadelphia: U. of Pennsylvania Press, 1957).

Input-Output

For a good survey of both theory and applications, see Hollis Chenery and Paul Clark, *Interindustry Economics* (New York: Wiley, 1959).

Firm and Industry

Useful descriptions and analyses of American industry can be found in Richard Caves, *American Industry: Structure, Conduct, Performance* (New York: Prentice-Hall [pb], 1964); Joe S. Bain, *Industrial Organization* (New York: Wiley, 1959); and Walter Adams, *Structure of American Industry*, rev. ed. (New York: Macmillan, 1961). For enterprise decision making, see Dow Votaw, *Modern Corporations* (New York: Prentice-Hall [pb], 1965); Robin Marris, *The Economic Theory of "Managerial Capitalism"* (London: Macmillan, 1964); and William Fellner, *Probability and Profit* (Homewood, Ill.: Irwin, 1965). New treatments of the role of information in market decision making can be found in two recent papers by George Stigler in the *Journal of Political Economy*, "The Economics of Information" (June 1961), and "A Theory of Oligopoly" (February 1964).

Bargaining

The standard analytic work on the game theory that lies behind the analysis of bargaining is R. Duncan Luce and Howard Raiffa, *Games and Decisions* (New York: Wiley, 1957). Attempts to apply the theory can be found in Martin Shubik, *Strategy and Market Structure* (New York: Wiley, 1959). For a more popular account of bargaining, see Anatol Rapaport, *Fights, Games and Debates* (Ann Arbor: U. of Michigan Press, 1960).

Labor and Capital

A variety of analytic and policy issues relating to labor can be found in William Bowen (ed.), *Labor and the National Economy* (New York: Norton [pb], 1965); Richard Perlman (ed.), *Wage Determination, Market or Power Forces* (Boston: Heath [pb], 1964); and Albert Rees, *The Economics of Trade Unions* (Chicago: U. of Chicago Press [pb], 1962).

A classic, readable and still useful account of capital theory is Irving Fisher, *Theory of Interest* (New York: Macmillan, 1930). For a very succinct and lucid modern statement, see Robert M. Solow, *Capital Theory and the Rate of Return* (Chicago: Rand McNally, 1963).

Welfare and General Equilibrium

General equilibrium is nicely described in George Stigler, *Theory of Price*, 3rd ed. (New York: Macmillan, 1966). For a deeper look, see Robert Dorfman, Paul Samuelson and Robert Solow, *Linear Programming and Economic Analysis* (New York: McGraw-Hill, 1958). Chaps. 13 and 14. For statements of the basic propositions of welfare economics, see Tibor Scitovsky, *Welfare and Competition* (Chicago:

Irwin, 1951); and Tjalling Koopmans, *Three Essays on the State of Economic Sciences* (New York: McGraw-Hill, 1957), first essay. For a description of the changing legal framework of market decision making, see John R. Commons, *Legal Foundations of Capitalism* (Madison: U. of Wisconsin Press [pb], 1959, first published in 1924); and W. Friedmann, *Law in a Changing Society* (Berkeley: U. of California Press, 1959). On antitrust policy, see the books by Caves and Bain cited above and also Carl Kaysen and Donald Turner, *Antitrust Policy: An Economic and Legal Analysis* (Cambridge: Harvard U. P., 1959).

Index

INDEX